Moonshine Nation

Moonshine Nation

The Art of Creating Cornbread in a Bottle

MARK SPIVAK

LYONS PRESS
Guilford, Connecticut
An imprint of Globe Pequot Press

Lyons Press is an imprint of Globe Pequot Press.

Part opener jar photo by Kelsey Pouk

Editor: Amy Lyons
Project Editor: Meredith Dias
Text Design/Layout: Maggie Peterson

Library of Congress Cataloging-in-Publication Data

Spivak, Mark (Mark Allen), author.
 Moonshine nation : the art of creating cornbread in a bottle / Mark Spivak.
    pages cm
 Summary: "Moonshine Nation is the story of Moonshine's history and
origins alongside profiles of modern moonshiners (and a collection of
drinks from each)"— Provided by publisher.
 ISBN 978-0-7627-9702-8 (paperback)
1. Distilling industries—Piedmont (U.S. : Region) 2.
Distilleries—Piedmont (U.S. : Region) 3. Distilling, Illicit—Piedmont
(U.S. : Region)—History. I. Title.
 TP590.6.U6S65 2014
 338.4'7663500973—dc23

                                                                    2014011011

Printed in the United States of America

10 9 8 7 6 5 4 3 2 1

For Carolann

All roads, rivers, and hurricanes

Contents

Introduction

Like many consumers, I believed that bourbon was the true American spirit. It's a good story, and distillers in Kentucky are adept at telling it. Bourbon, however, is basically aged corn whiskey, and corn whiskey was made in this country from the earliest days of the colonial settlers: Scots-Irish immigrants who traveled to the New World and brought their distilling skills with them. After the Whiskey Rebellion of 1791–94, those folks went underground and concocted their product in thousands of improvised stills throughout the Appalachian South. Their whiskey—unregulated, untaxed, and illegal—was made by the light of the moon and became known as moonshine.

As I researched the Whiskey Rebellion, I realized it was the source of many of the social and cultural divisions we see in America today. The widespread mistrust of the government throughout the South, as well as the resentment of the moneyed classes on the part of hardworking, rural citizens, is directly traceable to the events of 1791–94. Moonshining in the Appalachian South became both a source of sustenance and a way of life. In addition to being the only way to survive, it also became a symbol of the individual's resistance against forces beyond his or her control.

Moonshine today is legal in many states, and mason jars filled with corn whiskey populate the shelves of retail stores across the country. Even so, the attitudes of moonshiners haven't changed much. Many of these men and women are descendants of generations of people who hid stills in remote spots in the backwoods and risked prison time to support their families. They are proud of their heritage and are committed to making sure that their ancestors' way of life doesn't disappear.

The first part of this book traces the history of moonshine from the Whiskey Rebellion through the tax wars of the nineteenth century, and onward to Prohibition toward the present day. The second half consists of profiles of latter-day, legal moonshiners. These people welcomed me into their houses, sheds, and distilleries, shared their stories and their hospitality, and I'm grateful for it: It gave me a glimpse into a freewheeling period of American history that is now being glamorized in popular culture. As I listened, I realized that many of the memories were bittersweet. Moonshining and bootlegging were hard and dangerous work; while a handful of people did get rich, most were engaged in a desperate effort to eke out a living.

The widespread appeal of moonshine today goes way beyond the product itself. Certainly, most modern moonshine is far better than the illegal corn whiskey once produced in backwoods stills. More importantly, it symbolizes a lost America—a place free of commutes and urban blight, where people can defy the system and occasionally make the authorities look ridiculous. As I note in my profile of notorious moonshiner Popcorn Sutton, we all yearn at times to be the guy sticking his middle finger at society, and immersing ourselves in their stories helps us to play out that fantasy in our minds.

Of course, the current popularity of moonshine is connected to more than myth. Modern distillers are turning out a pure and carefully crafted product, and one that is extremely mixable. For those who want something to sip on, many flavored moonshines are delightful, especially since producers have become pickier about the quality of the fruit used for their infusions.

Most importantly—for me, at least—is the fact that these are simply great stories. I hope I've done them justice. Open a mason jar, make yourself comfortable, and settle in for some amazing tales.

Part 1:

LEGACY AND LEGEND

☆ ☆ ☆

MARCHING ON PENNSYLVANIA

In October 1794, a force of thirteen thousand troops prepared for war in western Pennsylvania. President George Washington had raised the federal expedition, which was larger than many of the armies he led into battle during the Revolutionary War. They marched forward, prepared to put down an insurrection that threatened the sovereignty of the United States—an uprising that had become known as the Whiskey Rebellion.

There was only one problem: The enemy we were about to confront was us. The president was marching the army to go to war with American citizens.

How did this astonishing situation come about?

In the aftermath of the Revolution, the new government of the United States was deeply in debt. When the Washington administration took office in 1789, that debt was slightly over $52 million, or roughly $1.3 billion in today's dollars—not $16 trillion, to be sure, but a sum that the infant democracy found to be disturbing. The individual states were unwilling to repay their share of it. Aside from retiring that debt, the main goal of the new administration was to consolidate power under the umbrella of the federal government. Washington wanted to make the country he had founded into an institution that was truly the United States of America, rather than a collection of formerly rebellious colonies.

Alexander Hamilton, his ambitious secretary of the treasury, came up with a twofold plan. The first stage involved something called assumption: The new national government would assume responsibility for the debts incurred by the states during the war, thus ensuring that the states were permanently obligated to the nation. To pay for that assumption of debt, he proposed an excise tax on whiskey. This would not only retire the debt, but

Protesters tar and feather a federal revenue agent during the Whiskey Rebellion, 1794. PUBLIC DOMAIN

Moonshine Nation

also pave the way for the ultimate sovereignty of the government, legitimizing its ability to tax citizens for anything and everything. It was a touchy and explosive idea, since the impetus for the American Revolution had been the unfair taxation imposed on the colonies by England.

Even at this early point in the emerging American democracy, there was a gulf between hardworking farmers and entrepreneurs and the rich, privileged class. The Revolution had been fomented by wealthy merchants, after all, men who found their ability to conduct free trade hampered by King George, and the farmers and citizens in the countryside had basically come along with them. To make matters worse, the war debt was owed to those same moneyed interests, investors who lived in the cities of the Northeast. Out on the boundaries of the frontier—which at this time was western Pennsylvania—settlers were engaged in a desperate struggle to survive, a life that was very different from the one lived by their countrymen on the Eastern Seaboard. In imposing the whiskey tax, Hamilton was basically telling the working class that they had to pay for the redemption of the rich.

From the beginning of the Revolution, Pennsylvania was the most extreme of the colonies in its advocacy of the rights of workers, small farmers, and common people against the interests of wealthy landowners and industrialists. Its state constitution, adopted in 1776, included such previously unheard-of measures as allowing poor people the right to vote and hold office. It was a warning shot to the more conservative and traditional colonies, such as Massachusetts, that they intended to make life difficult for moneyed interests in the new nation.

Along with prominent investors, Hamilton conducted a lengthy and complex campaign to bring about national taxation—a crusade that lasted more than a decade, as he tried to convince Congress to usurp the rights of the states to levy taxes on their citizens. He even went so far as to encourage a movement that would reverse the Revolution and stage a military coup. At the end of the war, both officers and men had not been paid for five years, and no one knew where the money would come from, or if the back salaries would be paid at all. Hamilton saw the potential revolt of the army as the catalyst that would force the government to take control of the national purse strings. The result was the Newburgh crisis of 1782, which was eventually neutralized by George Washington—but not before the principle of federal authority over taxation was realized. In the end the officers were paid but the men were not, and the nation was populated by impoverished war veterans who felt the government had taken advantage of them.

Those destitute veterans increasingly moved westward, to areas such as Pennsylvania where they could thrive and prosper outside the realm of government influence. There were large tracts of mountain land they could occupy as squatters, refusing to pay rent to the landlords in the east. One of these landlords, ironically, was George Washington, who had purchased nearly sixty thousand acres of western land as a speculative investment prior to the Revolution. There was little that men such as Washington could do about it. America in the eighteenth century was a wild and unsettled place, a land that lacked an organized police force and where travel was uncertain and treacherous. The squatters could hide out in the woods, making a living as subsistence farmers.

They augmented their income by indulging in the one trade their Scots-Irish heritage had prepared them for: making whiskey.

No wonder, then, that the whiskey tax—shepherded through Congress in 1791 by Alexander Hamilton, the first secretary of the treasury—was a particular outrage to home distillers scattered throughout the western frontier. During his efforts to pass the tax, Hamilton made no secret of the fact that it would be enforced by a cadre of powerful federal agents. It was enacted in March 1791, and was undoubtedly seen by the well-heeled members of Congress as a favorable alternative to a tax on land or wealth.

Hamilton's theory of the whiskey tax, at least as it was presented to Congress, was simple. According to him, whiskey was a luxury item; as such, it was consumed by the moneyed classes, who could easily afford to have the tax passed along to them. This was untrue, of course. Whiskey consumption in early America was widespread among the entire population, but Hamilton's theory seemed to provide the politicians with safe cover.

Not only was whiskey the drink of choice, but it also formed the basis of income for many small farmers. In eighteenth-century America, transportation of freight over land was slow, painful, and expensive. You might be able to sell a ton of grain or corn in a town fifty miles away, but you couldn't get it there. Transform that grain or corn into whiskey, and the journey became possible.

Hamilton structured the whiskey tax to give producers two alternatives: a per-gallon levy or a flat fee. The flat fee obviously favored large-scale distillers, allowing them to sell whiskey more cheaply than their counterparts in the countryside. William Hogeland, in his book *The Whiskey Rebellion*, speculates that one of

Hamilton's goals was to concentrate production in the hands of the large distillers. This would stimulate the creation of an industrial farming system to supply the stills and eventually allow America to morph into an economic power that would rival England.

Whatever the real reasons behind it, the whiskey tax created outrage among the rural population that exceeded any previous anger they had felt toward King George. At the time, the American frontier was defined as lying west of the Appalachians, in the Allegheny Valley of Pennsylvania and the Carolina mountains. From the point of view of settlers in these areas, the new government they had helped to create was engaged in a power grab that made independence seem worthless. After fighting the Revolution for seven years, they were back where they had started, with one advantage: Having fought their oppressors once and won, they were confident they could do it again.

Shortly after the passage of the whiskey tax, General John Neville was appointed to collect the tax in Pennsylvania. Although Neville lived in the region and had fought in the Revolutionary War, he was a symbol of the moneyed classes that many small farmers hated. His plantation, Bower Hill, stood on a promontory above the Monongahela River and sprawled over ten thousand acres. He began organizing his forces, and the resistance organized as well.

The collection effort did not get off to a promising start. In September 1791 Robert Johnson, Neville's supervisor of revenue for Washington and Allegheny Counties, was tarred and feathered by an angry mob. An official sent to serve warrants on Johnson's attackers was whipped, tarred, and feathered as well. The federal response was sluggish and disorganized for the rest of 1791 and well into 1792. In May of that year, Hamilton engineered a revision to the tax law that tightened restrictions up and down the supply chain.

Hamilton was gradually coming to the position that the only way to put down the resistance was by armed federal force. To succeed in that goal, he needed to get President Washington on his side. His relationship with Washington had been difficult and complicated for quite a long time. In the early days of the Revolutionary War, Hamilton had maneuvered himself into the post of Washington's chief of staff. Their working life had been stormy, and Hamilton eventually resigned from Washington's staff in protest, but they had maintained a cautious professional dance in the years since. When Washington took office in 1789 and appointed Hamilton as his treasury secretary, their dynamic was what it had always been: Neither man liked or trusted the other, but Washington recognized that Hamilton's brilliance was essential to the nation's future.

Hamilton now began pressing the president to take action, although some Cabinet members—notably Edmund Randolph, the attorney general—were opposed to the idea. For his part, Washington was ambivalent. While he supported the idea of a strong and sovereign federal government, he was reluctant to use military force against his fellow citizens. Hamilton drafted a proclamation condemning organized resistance to the whiskey tax, and Washington signed it in September 1792. Posturing aside, the tax was not being collected, and it would remain uncollected for a long time to come.

The resistance was growing. One month before Hamilton's proclamation, a convention had met in Pittsburgh to coalesce opposition to the whiskey tax. The convention was dominated by members of the Mingo Creek Association, a militia group that had agitated on behalf of the government before and during the Revolution. They demanded the repeal of the tax and the resignation of Neville, and promised to retaliate against any citizen who helped the government enforce the law.

The tax remained largely uncollected into 1793, and Neville was finding it increasingly difficult to hire anyone to work for him. He ultimately decided to take a personal role in the collection effort. Neville rented space in a tavern in Washington County and set up the first federal excise office in the area. The Mingo Creek Association responded by terrorizing the tavern owner and destroying the building.

By early 1794 the militants—no longer content with harassing tax collectors and collaborators—were burning down the barns of farmers who had registered their stills with the government. Neville was growing more insistent that troops be deployed to Pennsylvania to help him out. The government sent David Lenox, a federal marshal, to the region to serve warrants on the recalcitrant distillers. Neville accompanied Lenox on his duties, and warning shots were fired at the two men. On July 16, members of the Mingo Creek Association came to Neville's plantation at Bower Hill and demanded the surrender of Lenox. A firefight ensued, and several rebels were killed. The following day, a rebel force of six hundred arrived at the house, and a full-scale battle erupted.

Neville escaped to Pittsburgh, but Bower Hill was burned to the ground.

At this point Washington was backed into a corner, and federal intervention seemed inevitable. The situation was dire. The rebels, now numbering in the thousands, were threatening secession from the United States; they had designed their own flag and promised the renewal of the Revolution. There was talk of burning the city of Pittsburgh. As seven thousand protesters gathered at Braddock's Field several miles outside the city, Washington called an emergency Cabinet meeting, and force was advocated by everyone except the attorney general.

According to the Militia Act of 1792, a Supreme Court justice had to certify that federal troops were necessary to resolve lawlessness in one of the states. In an effort to buy time, Washington sent peace emissaries to Pennsylvania, and negotiations began with both rebels and local moderates. On August 4, 1794, Justice James Wilson gave the government its certification. Washington called up militias from New Jersey, Maryland, Virginia, and eastern Pennsylvania, assembling his force of thirteen thousand—an overwhelmingly large army for the time. In October, while peace negotiations still continued, the president traveled to Pennsylvania to review the troops.

It was the first, and perhaps the only, time an American president prepared to lead troops into battle against his countrymen. Washington reportedly had no enthusiasm for it. He was sixty-two in 1794, a relatively advanced age at that period, and was in constant pain from a back injury that had occurred a few years earlier. His personal involvement in a military expedition had been advocated by Hamilton as far back as 1792, and Washington was well aware of the powerful symbolism of his trip to Pennsylvania. His presence at the front would certainly inspire the army and strike fear into the rebels.

In fact, the president had no intention of staying at the front, much less mounting a horse and leading the charge to destroy the rebels. His peace delegates, who were still engaged in back-channel talks, reported to him that the insurrection was fizzling out. The moderates were gaining traction, since the law-abiding citizens of western Pennsylvania were terrified and anxious to make a deal; the leaders of the uprising were leaving the area, and many of their followers were fading back silently into the countryside. There was every sign that the rebellion would be over before it started. On October 21, after seventeen days of military parades and stirring speeches, Washington left western Pennsylvania and headed back east.

His attitude toward the uprising remained ambiguous. While he gave explicit instructions to Hamilton that the army should conduct itself in a legal manner, with no looting or reprisals, he also felt that there should be some "atonement" in the region for what had occurred. In practice, the aftermath was left up to Hamilton, who presided over the mass arrests of rebels. Many of the offenders were sentenced without trial. Thousands of others had already fled—the agitators may have been zealots, but few were crazy enough to believe they could defeat the US Army in battle.

Following the Whiskey Rebellion, as Hamilton was fond of calling it, order was restored and most of the local stills were registered. The tax remained difficult to collect, however, and was repealed after Thomas Jefferson took office in 1800, although it was to reappear in many forms in the years that followed. Washington tended to view the affair as a victory—not just for him personally, but also for the authority of the infant government. He may or may not have been justified in seeing it that way, but the three-year conflict never succeeded in raising the revenue that Hamilton thought the government desperately needed. If anything, the enormous expense of supplying the 1794 expedition put the administration further in the hole. They did receive a small amount of revenue from Washington himself: Perhaps intrigued by the economics of the conflict, the president decided to become a distiller. By 1798, the year before his death, his still at Mount Vernon produced eleven thousand gallons of whiskey and made a profit of $7,500 (the average yearly income at the time was about $300). Presumably he paid the tax, and we can also assume he opted for the flat rate.

From a military point of view, the government's actions during the uprising were baffling. On the surface they seemed to have triumphed: A massive display of federal force had caused the rebels to abandon their cause and flee. In reality, the previous three years on the frontier had been marked by mob rule. Bands of vigilantes had terrorized citizens, destroying property, beating and abusing federal agents, and operating in the open without fear of repression by authorities. They had conducted a highly successful guerrilla campaign against what they saw as the government's unfair policies; when the US Army finally showed up, the rebels disappeared and left thirteen thousand soldiers with nothing to do except play cards and clean their rifles. The situation was eerily similar to what was to occur nearly two centuries later in Vietnam, when a huge display of American military might could not defeat the guerrilla tactics of the Viet Cong. The enemy was simply fighting a different war, one that the US government didn't seem to comprehend.

The crucial legacy of the Whiskey Rebellion is that it never really ended. In western Pennsylvania, in the Appalachian hills and the North Carolina mountains, in the rural parts of Virginia and West Virginia, the values of the rebellion took hold and flourished. The most important of those values—the right of the individual to protest against the mandates of an unfair government, and the nobility of the laboring class compared to the moneyed elite— became articles of faith, beliefs passed on from generation to generation. And the owners of the small stills who refused to pay tax on their whiskey didn't go away. They went underground and became moonshiners.

☆ ☆ ☆

GENERAL GRANT'S WHISKEY

During his sixty-three years on the planet, Ulysses S. Grant experienced dizzying heights and very deep valleys. After graduating from West Point, he served as an officer for more than a decade and fought bravely in the Mexican-American War, only to resign in disgrace in 1854. As a civilian, he failed miserably at every business venture he tried. He rejoined the service after the Civil War began in 1861; after winning a string of brilliant victories, he was named commanding general of the Union army, and today is recognized as one of the greatest military strategists of all time. From 1869 to 1877, he was the eighteenth president of the United States.

According to most accounts, he was a drunk. Today we would classify Grant as a binge drinker, although the amount of whiskey required for one of his binges was very small: at five feet seven inches tall and 135 pounds, one or two drinks were sufficient to put him under the table. Although he had long periods of temperance, his stress-induced consumption of alcohol (or the reputation of it) haunted him for most of his life. There is no evidence that drinking had an adverse effect on his ability to command troops, but a string of jealous fellow officers called for his dismissal throughout the Civil War. After a series of these requests, Lincoln was rumored to have given his famous quote: "Find out what kind of whiskey he drinks," the president reportedly said, "so that I may send some of it to my other generals who are having so much trouble winning battles."

And it was whiskey that almost brought down the presidency of Ulysses S. Grant, although in that case a drop of it never even approached his lips.

In 1802 President Thomas Jefferson abolished the controversial excise tax on whiskey, the tax that had sparked the Whiskey Rebellion of 1791–94. The action was symbolic, since the tax had been largely uncollected for most of its existence. The United States of the time did not lend itself to an organized system of federal law enforcement. There were few roads; travel by horseback was difficult in the best of times, nearly impossible in bad weather, and it took days to travel from one town to another. Federal revenue agents might call for the voluntary registration of stills, but they lacked the ability to hunt down moonshiners in remote rural locations.

The whiskey tax was revived briefly to pay for the War of 1812 but remained dormant for nearly fifty years after that. In the interim, the distilling industry began to undergo changes.

Rectifiers appeared on the scene—businessmen who built large stills in cities, then bought up whiskey from small farmers and processed it into a uniform product. If you had a small still located within a day's horseback ride of Louisville or Atlanta, this arrangement made sense. Out in the Appalachian hills, however,

A classic moonshine still in the Appalachian hills. PUBLIC DOMAIN

the production of moonshine continued without pause, and whiskey actually functioned as currency in many rural areas.

With the outbreak of the Civil War, Abraham Lincoln desperately needed to raise revenue. The US national debt was $64.8 million in 1861; four years later, it had ballooned to a staggering $2.6 billion. To cover the shortfall, the government enacted a series of taxes. These included a first-ever income tax, which met with surprisingly little resistance, since payment was viewed as a patriotic act by most citizens in the North. The whiskey tax was revived again, of course, although it was modest at first—around 20 cents per gallon. By 1864 it had risen to slightly more than $2 per gallon, or the rough equivalent of more than $30 in 2014 dollars.

There was only one problem. The newly formed Confederacy included all of the major whiskey-producing states, places such as Georgia, Virginia, Tennessee, and the Carolinas, even though the manufacture of illegal moonshine had already been raised to a fine art in those states. The only major distilling state still loyal to the Union was Kentucky, and the market was not yet dominated by the large producers that would emerge toward the end of the nineteenth century. True, companies such as Jim Beam, Early Times, and Old Crow (Grant's favorite) did exist, although much of the whiskey was made by farmers up in the hills—or, more precisely, their wives, since the men had gone off to fight the war. Even though the large distillers did not yet dominate the state, as they would later on, some sources estimate that the contribution of whiskey taxation to the Union economy might have been as high as 40 percent.

Strangely, it never seemed to occur to the Confederacy to impose a tax on whiskey, even though they were as desperate for war funds as the Union. At the start of the conflict, the Southern government was primarily financed by tariffs on imports and exports, but that revenue stream dried up after the Union blockade of Confederate ports and the ill-advised Southern strategy of withholding cotton from Europe in the hope of gaining diplomatic recognition. In any case, the collection of taxes from illegal moonshiners would have been nearly impossible, and there was no manpower to collect it.

In 1872, during the administration of Ulysses S. Grant, most of the Civil War taxes were rescinded. The whiskey tax remained, however, and would stay in place until the advent of Prohibition in 1920. In the intervening years, the temperance movement swelled to the status of a national crusade, but liquor was still vitally important to the government—according to most estimates, it formed virtually one-third of all federal revenue. The situation changed with the reenactment of the national income tax in 1913. Once the bulk of the government's funds came from a place other than alcohol taxes, Prohibition was a sure thing.

Hiram Ulysses Grant was born in Ohio in 1822. He was a mediocre student, but displayed an affinity for horses from an early age; you might call him a nineteenth-century version of a horse whisperer, although whispering was probably not one of his training methods. When Grant was seventeen, his father, Jesse, who was in the tannery business, announced that he was sending him to West Point. Grant had little enthusiasm for a military career, but would not have thought of defying his father. At that time, only a fraction of West Point graduates stayed in the army past their mandatory one year tour of duty; the Academy was one of two schools that trained their students to be civil engineers, and then—as now—it was a valuable education to have. The Congressman who sent his appointment to the War Department mistakenly recorded his name as Ulysses S. Grant, and the moniker stuck with him for the rest of his life.

At West Point he excelled in nothing more than horsemanship, graduating twenty-first out of thirty-nine in the class of 1843. He entered the infantry as a second lieutenant and fought valiantly in the Mexican-American War—a war with which he disagreed vehemently. Grant believed that the Mexican conflict was a ploy to add more slave states to the Union, and later felt that the South's secession was directly related to the American government's Mexican adventure. Still, it was an important learning experience. He served under General Zachary Taylor, Old Rough and Ready, who became Grant's model for generalship during the Civil War. He also worked as a quartermaster, which proved crucial later on in determining the level of supplies necessary to sustain a major army. He fought with and met many officers he would encounter in the Civil War, including Robert E. Lee. In 1848 Grant married his longtime sweetheart, Julia Dent.

After the war Grant endured a series of postings to remote garrisons in California, which required long separations from his wife and children. His boredom and depression increased, as did his drinking, which had surfaced during the war but never became a serious issue. He began to talk of leaving the army, although he was concerned about the economic impact on his family of giving up a secure income. In April 1854, he abruptly resigned his commission.

Jean Edward Smith, in his biography of Grant, gives the following version of events. Grant was observed to be drunk on numerous occasions while on duty. Lt. Col. Robert C. Buchanan, his commanding officer, gave him the choice of resigning or facing a court martial. Grant resigned immediately. Ironically, Buchanan was later to serve under Grant during the Civil War.

The civilian world was not kind to Grant. His father, Jesse, who was disappointed with his son's resignation, observed that "he will be poorly qualified for the pursuits of private life." Jesse was entirely correct. Grant spent most of the next seven years in a state of severe poverty, hamstrung by his total lack of judgment in human nature. He first failed as a farmer and suffered severe losses in the Panic of 1857. He then went into partnership in a real estate business, which also failed. He finally swallowed his pride and asked his father for a job in the family tannery, a business he had sworn never to enter. He did a competent job at the tannery, and his drinking remained under control; he probably would have stayed there for the rest of his working life but for an extraordinary turn of events.

Toward the end of 1860, Abraham Lincoln was elected president on an antislavery platform. The response from the outraged Southern states was immediate. On December 20, South Carolina seceded from the Union, followed by Mississippi

(January 9), Florida (January 10), Alabama (January 11), Georgia (January 19), Louisiana (January 26), and Texas (February 1). On April 12 the guns of General Beauregard's forces fired on Fort Sumter, and the war had begun.

Lincoln put out a call for seventy-five thousand volunteers, and Grant received permission from his father to return to the army. His rise was meteoric. After an early series of victories, his troops seized control of the Mississippi River and split the Confederate forces in half. Lincoln gave him command of the entire Union army in late 1863, and on April 9, 1865, he accepted Lee's surrender at Appomattox.

Historians have advanced many theories about Grant's dramatic reversal of fortune during the Civil War, but no one has been able to adequately explain how he went from being a complete bum to one of the most celebrated figures in history in slightly less than four years. His path to greatness was not completely without obstacles: Grant was ambitious and at times overeager, and allegations of drunkenness haunted him throughout the conflict. His attacks on the Confederacy were relentless, his casualty figures were alarmingly high, and many people thought of him as a butcher. Still, it was difficult not to view the situation as one in which the man and the moment were perfectly matched. Many of the character flaws that had haunted him in civilian life seemed to have no bearing on his second military career—although his excessive loyalty toward subordinates, coupled with a tendency to trust the wrong people, proved disastrous when he became a civilian once again.

Were it not for the assassination of Lincoln in 1865, Grant would likely have been remembered simply as a great general. He was idolized throughout the entire country and treated as the nineteenth-century equivalent of a rock star. Initially he worked closely with President Andrew Johnson, but soon quarreled with the new president over his Reconstruction policies; Johnson, for his part, considered Grant to be a potential rival in the coming election of 1868. He proved to be right. Grant secured the Republican nomination and was elected in a landslide, eerily foreshadowing the experience of Dwight Eisenhower in 1952.

Even though Grant's eight years as president are generally viewed as a catastrophe, the truth is that he had many positive accomplishments. He championed the rights of the freed slaves, completed the work of Reconstruction, and went to war with the Ku Klux Klan. He advocated government reform, opposed patronage, and established the Civil Service Commission in 1871. This last action was ironic, in view of the fact that Grant's administration was rife with nepotism—according to some estimates, he had over three dozen family members on the federal payroll. His Cabinet was composed of incompetent and corrupt cronies, men whom Grant defended even after it became obvious that they had no interests at heart other than their own. Even though his personal reputation for honesty and integrity remained high, virtually every single department of his government was plagued by scandal.

The list of controversies included Black Friday (an economic collapse caused by gold speculators, who were later linked to

Grant), the New York Custom House Ring (involving two of his appointees), the Star Route Postal Ring (bribery for postal contracts), the Delano Affair (in which the secretary of the interior allegedly took bribes in exchange for land grants), Pratt & Boyd (a company that reportedly bribed the attorney general to escape prosecution), the Trading Post Ring (wherein the war secretary supposedly took bribes in exchange for military contracts), and Cattelism (involving Cattell and Company, accused of bribing the secretary of the navy for navy contracts). This is only a partial list. The most damaging scandal, however, was the Whiskey Ring.

Throughout the decade after Lincoln reinstated the whiskey tax, there were rumors of widespread collusion between distillers and revenue agents. In fact, the situation was worse than anyone imagined: Large distillers routinely bribed financially strapped agents to overlook a large part of their production. Press reports estimated that between twelve and fifteen million gallons of whiskey were untaxed as a result. In 1875 Grant encouraged his newly appointed treasury secretary, Benjamin Bristow, to target the chain of corruption. His initial instructions to the secretary were totally in line with his character: "Let no guilty man escape if it can be avoided." Bristow, a zealous reformer, was happy to comply. He set up a sting operation that resulted in 350 indictments and the uncovering of nearly $4 million in uncollected whiskey taxes.

If the affair had ended there, Grant would have been a hero. However, his innate ability to trust and defend the wrong people allowed him to snatch defeat from the jaws of victory. The weak point in this particular chain was Orville E. Babcock, Grant's private secretary for the preceding seven years, who sat directly outside the Oval Office and had the president's complete trust. Although the evidence against Babcock was circumstantial, much of it suggested that he was up to his armpits in the scandal. Grant vigorously defended his subordinate and went so far as to give a deposition on Babcock's behalf during the 1876 trial. (His advisors persuaded him not to testify in person.)

The situation deteriorated from there. Grant appointed a special prosecutor, John B. Henderson, who had been a severe critic of the administration while he was in the Senate. Henderson eventually accused Grant of interfering with Bristow's investigation, and Grant fired him, in yet another bizarre foreshadowing of history: Richard Nixon's firing of Watergate special prosecutor Archibald Cox in 1973. Babcock was ultimately acquitted, but rumors swirled around Grant for the remainder of his second term. There were accusations that he was personally involved in the Whiskey Ring, and had even used some of the funds to finance his 1872 reelection campaign. Grant's loyalty to his subordinates unnecessarily tarnished his reputation, and he was not the first—or the last—president to be nearly brought down by whiskey.

Up in the hills, things were getting tense. Economic conditions were desperate throughout the South in the wake of the Civil War, and many farmers needed the extra income from moonshine simply to survive. The Treasury Department's Revenue Bureau was established in 1876, and gradually morphed into a national police force dedicated to seeking out moonshiners, arresting them, and destroying their stills. The moonshiners fought back, declaring war on the revenuers and persecuting those who collaborated with them; they enlisted the KKK to help them fight the federal menace. In Georgia alone, over 75 percent of court cases involved illegal alcohol, and gun battles (as well as fatalities) between the opposing sides were common.

The problem was exacerbated by the fact that taxes on liquor were going up, fueled in part by the growing temperance movement. They eased somewhat after the Civil War, but by the end of the nineteenth century they stood at $1.10 per gallon, or once again the equivalent of $30 in modern money. Temperance advocates believed that, by setting taxes high, they would discourage public consumption of alcohol. Nothing could be further from the truth. As we'll see in the chapter on Baptists and bootleggers, raising the price of legal whiskey simply made moonshine seem more appealing to a broad slice of the population. America was caught in a spiral, one which would eventually create a booming underground industry and fuel the growth of organized crime.

☆ ☆ ☆

ROBIN HOOD OF THE DARK CORNER

Legends die hard, but few have been as long-lasting or universally appealing as Robin Hood. The image of the outlaw as folk hero first began to surface during the Middle Ages. Forget that the story is spun to children early on, and that the concept has been the basis for innumerable ballads, novels, cartoons, and full-length feature films. Robin Hood is a hard tale to resist.

After a number of centuries, an extra thread was added: the hero that steals from the rich and gives to the poor. This offers something for everyone. It allows rich people to perform involuntary acts of charity, which they may secretly feel good about while publicly complaining that they have been robbed. The poor can benefit from the illicit redistribution of wealth, without themselves doing anything morally or legally wrong.

The history of moonshine is filled with Robin Hood figures, but few are more compelling than "Major" Lewis R. Redmond. Born in 1854, he was so legendary that a romance novel and a book-length biography were written about him before he was thirty. After a brief and colorful career in North Carolina, he fled over the border to South Carolina's Dark Corner, where he became even more of a folk hero, and embellished the fame of that region in the process.

In one sense the legend of Lewis Redmond was probably exaggerated: During his lifetime, and in his time and place, there were very few rich people to steal from. The economic devastation throughout the South after the Civil War was severe and widespread. Most of the cities had been leveled, and the agricultural system of the countryside had been destroyed. In retrospect, Grant's surrender terms at Appomattox were both generous and prescient. By allowing the Confederate soldiers to take their horses and pack animals home with them, so that they might have all available help in raising a crop, he acknowledged that the coming winter would be a hard one.

It was harder than anyone imagined, and became no easier in the decades ahead. In the popular mind, the Southern economy had been based on the slave system and would have been impossible to maintain without the large plantations where cotton was grown and harvested. In fact, only a small minority of Southerners were prosperous enough to own slaves. Plantations such as Tara in *Gone with the Wind* certainly existed, but they were very far from the reality of most whites in the region.

Northern schoolchildren are taught that Reconstruction would have succeeded were it not for the assassination of Abraham Lincoln. More than likely, the process of reuniting the Southern states with the Union would have been impossible regardless of who occupied the White House. Aside from the humiliation

"Law and Moonshine—Crooked Whiskey in North Carolina" (*Harper's Weekly,* 1879). PUBLIC DOMAIN

of defeat and the shattering of their traditional culture, most Southerners now saw the federal government as a foreign power treading on their soil. In one sense they were correct: Troops of the Union army occupied most of the South until 1877.

Many rural Southerners were dirt farmers, desperately poor and trying to scratch a living from the land; they were isolated from their fellow citizens in towns and cities as well. This isolation reached its peak in areas such as South Carolina's Dark Corner, located in the western part of the state along the Blue Ridge Mountains. Although the region encompassed parts of Spartanburg and Pickens Counties, the center of the Dark Corner was the northern segment of Greenville County, around Glassy Mountain Township and Hogback Mountain. The area had been settled by Scots-Irish immigrants in the late 1700s and had evolved into a stronghold of Appalachian culture. Parts of it were no more than thirty miles from the city of Greenville, but it was a world apart. Cotton farming was out of the question due to the mountainous topography, so most farmers grew grains and corn, and followed the time-honored custom of turning those crops into moonshine. By the 1840s the area had already gained a reputation for backwardness, drunkenness, and violence, particularly among the more genteel citizens of Greenville.

To the residents of the Dark Corner, it hardly mattered if the rest of the South was suffering in the aftermath of the Civil War. Life changed little for them, regardless of anything that might be happening in the outside world. For them the events of 1861–1865 were occurring on the surface of the water, and they were at the bottom of the ocean floor: The effects of the war reached them as echoes of distant ripples. In fact, area farmers were not particularly supportive of the Confederate cause, and very few enlisted; later in the conflict the Dark Corner served as a haven for deserters.

For these farmers the crucially important event was the reinstatement of the whiskey tax in 1862 and the permanent enactment of that tax in 1866, along with the creation of the Office of the Commissioner of Internal Revenue and its network of enforcement. From their point of view, the federal government had always been a foreign power exercising illegal authority over their fortunes. The practice of distilling and selling moonshine, after all, was a custom that predated the establishment of the United States of America.

The region was known for widespread violence. The law rarely penetrated into the Appalachian hills, and residents typically took matters into their own hands. Shootings were common, and homicides were frequent. Citizens who took advantage of the informer's fee to tip off the revenue agents about nearby stills were routinely killed, as were those suspected of being informers. John C. Campbell, an early student of the region, found that homicide rates in the Appalachian Mountains were among the highest in the country.

Violence increased dramatically after the Civil War. The attempts by federal agents to collect the whiskey tax, coupled with the occupation by the Union army, sparked the South Carolina Revenue Wars of 1866–1878. The period consisted of a prolonged series of armed skirmishes in which many members of both sides were slaughtered; enforcing the revenue laws turned out to be costly in both blood and treasure.

It was into this atmosphere that the outlaw Lewis Redmond rode in March 1876, as he crossed the state line into Pickens County.

Lewis Richard Redmond was born in April 1854 and grew up in rural western North Carolina. Although too young to fight in the Civil War, he liked to hang out at a neighboring Confederate base, where soldiers gave him the affectionate nickname of "Major." He probably learned to make moonshine as a child, and by the 1870s he was earning extra money by hauling payloads of illegal whiskey to market. His activities drew the attention of federal agents in the area, who issued a warrant for his arrest. Redmond wasn't home when the agents arrived at his house, so they arrested his father and transported him to Asheville. Redmond later popularized the story that the shock and strain of the arrest was responsible for the death of his elderly parents, although this was likely untrue.

On March 1, 1876, Redmond was transporting a load of whiskey along a country road when he was apprehended by Deputy US Marshal Alfred Duckworth. According to legend, Duckworth held Redmond at gunpoint while reading the warrant to him. Redmond assured him that he would go peacefully if Duckworth put away his pistol. As the marshal lowered his weapon, Redmond produced a hidden derringer and shot Duckworth through the throat. The officer died shortly afterward.

Redmond's father had lived in Pickens County during the 1830s, and Redmond believed that the people of the Dark Corner would be sympathetic to him and his cause. He was absolutely correct. There ensued a prolonged game of cat and mouse that persisted until 1881, when he was finally brought to justice. The locals supported him every step of the way; in their view someone who murdered a federal revenue agent in the line of duty was doing God's work. Redmond settled into the area and became intimate with Adeline Ladd, whom he married in 1878.

The sympathies of the locals intensified after the events of January 1877. A band of agents arrested Redmond and his future brother-in-law, Amos Ladd. Redmond escaped and was able

Alfred Duckworth, the federal marshal
Redmond killed in 1876. PUBLIC DOMAIN

to free Ladd in an ambush. About a week later agents raided Ladd's house and killed him without warning, further inflaming sentiment around the countryside. Redmond was well on his way to becoming a hero, and was already being referred to as a modern-day Robin Hood. He was certainly generous with his whiskey, but there's no clear evidence that he gave financial aid to his fellow moonshiners—although he did help them out in other ways. In March 1878 he helped spring three fellow moonshiners from the Pickens County jail, which further embellished his reputation.

President Grant had sent federal reinforcements to the region to settle things down, and Green Raum, the newly appointed commissioner of the Bureau of Internal Revenue, used maximum force in an attempt to bring law and order to the area. Nothing seemed to work. In the aftermath of the jailbreak, Raum dispatched a posse of one hundred men to catch Redmond, but they could not apprehend him. Redmond's legend grew. In the summer of 1878 the *Charleston News and Courier* ran a lengthy interview with the outlaw. It was conducted by a reporter named C. McKinley, who was no fan of the Bureau of Internal Revenue, and portrayed Redmond as an honest, devoted family man who had been unjustly persecuted by the government. In 1879 Bishop Edward Crittenden wrote *The Entwined Lives of Miss Gabrielle Austin and Redmond, The Outlaw,* an enormously popular dime novel (most of which was fabricated) that cast Redmond as a cross between Zorro and Lawrence of Arabia. Raum did make some progress in the summer of 1878 when he promised amnesty to local moonshiners if they pled guilty in federal court and agreed not to distill illegal liquor again, but Redmond's supporters were again outraged when they realized that the amnesty didn't extend to him.

Redmond was finally captured in April 1881, after a shootout with agents that left him seriously wounded. The government declined to prosecute him for the murder of Duckworth, and instead focused on violations of internal revenue laws. He was brought to trial in August, pled guilty, and was sentenced to ten years in the federal penitentiary in Auburn, New York.

In a book titled *Used to Be a Rough Place in Them Hills,* Joshua Beau Blackwell presents a nostalgic view of life in the Dark Corner. Blackwell is a native South Carolinian, the great-grandson of a moonshiner, who grew up listening to stories about the good old days. He now teaches history, and the book is "partly a reflection of my regret of the loss of a world long since past."

Blackwell isolates five key elements of Appalachian culture found in the Dark Corner: "a permanent yeoman economy based on agriculture; fewer restrictions on a woman's role in society; unique speech patterns; culturally accepted violence often linked to illicit alcohol; the blood feud." He laments the loss of the wilderness to "gated-community development." While it's not hard to bash the homogenization of contemporary society, it's also easy to sit in an air-conditioned house, well-fed and economically secure, and regret the loss of a culture that was spawned out of a desperate struggle to survive. Were the residents of the Dark Corner better off when they lived without electricity or running water, constantly looking over their shoulders for revenue agents, in an atmosphere of casual violence and murder? It's not clear if Blackwell thinks so, and unfortunately his ancestors aren't around to answer the question.

Still, strong memories persist of life and death in the Dark Corner. Writers such as Blackwell talk about blood feuds, but it wasn't all Hatfields and McCoys. For those not involved in moonshining, informing on others was frequently the easiest way to make a living, but it was also the most common way to get yourself killed. Above all else, the predominant belief in the area was that you had the right to do whatever you wanted on your own land. "The resulting mentality of the community was that crimes were not crimes," writes Blackwell, "but defense of natural rights being infringed upon by outsiders."

Although most historians believe the South Carolina Revenue Wars ended in 1878, they actually continued in one form or another well into the twentieth century. Initially revenue agents had the assistance of federal troops, but things became more difficult for them after the army occupation ended in 1877. Robert M. Wallace, the US Marshal for South Carolina, estimated that 80 percent of court expenses went toward trying moonshine cases. If anything, the violence became worse. As the nineteenth century came to a close, places like the Dark Corner were even more isolated and dangerous.

In the meantime the South was changing. A new wave of industrialization engulfed the region, encouraged by leaders who realized that the South's lack of industrial production was one of the main reasons they had lost the Civil War. As outside capital began to filter into places like Greenville, it became necessary to project a clean, healthy image of the area to investors. The specter of murderous, rampaging hillbillies up in the mountains was not an appealing one that was good for business.

In addition, the temperance movement was rapidly sweeping the nation. A chapter of the Women's Christian Temperance Union was established in Greenville in 1884. It was true that the country was increasingly drying up, but even worse than the concept of moonshiners up in the hills—from the perspective of someone thinking of building a factory—was the idea of a town's work force perpetually getting drunk on the stuff. Areas such as the Dark Corner were simply an embarrassment to communities such as Greenville, which were struggling to achieve respectability.

It took a long time for the production of illegal moonshine to disappear in the Dark Corner. The region began to open up during World War I, when Glassy Mountain Township was the headquarters of the artillery training base at Camp Wadsworth. However, Prohibition gave the moonshiners a second act. It was really not until well after World War II that things changed, due to an influx of outsiders moving in and shattering the area's traditional isolation.

And what of Major Lewis R. Redmond? In May 1884, President Chester Arthur granted him a full and unconditional pardon at the request of US Attorney General Benjamin Brewster and South Carolina senator (and former governor) Wade Hampton. Redmond returned to his wife and children, but not to moonshining. In 1886, believe it or not, he was hired to run a government distillery. He quickly became known for making the finest corn whiskey on the market, and his picture ended up on the label. He died in 1906, having spent the last two decades of his life making whiskey for the same government that had once dedicated its resources to hunting him down like a rabid dog.

☆ ☆ ☆

BAPTISTS AND BOOTLEGGERS

Western thinking is dualistic. Something is either true or it is not. We think in terms of either/or, yes or no, black or white. Most of us would be uncomfortable with the idea of two polar opposites working toward the same goal.

It's surprising, then, that a concept such as Baptists and bootleggers has found its way into our political thought. The idea is simple. Individuals or groups with totally conflicting philosophies find themselves supporting the same objectives; once achieved, the result is more than satisfactory to both sides.

The most frequently cited example of Baptists and bootleggers goes like this: Leaders of a deeply religious municipality feel strongly that their fellow citizens should not be consuming alcohol. After much effort, they manage to pass a law forbidding the purchase of any intoxicating beverages on Sundays. Bootleggers are delighted, since they now have a monopoly on the sale of booze one day a week. After a time, church leaders realize that consumption of illegal alcohol has skyrocketed on the Lord's day. The only possible solution, in their view, is stricter laws, and this leads to an escalating spiral in which more illicit hooch is sold. Both sides are now pleased: The bootleggers are getting rich, while the Baptists can deliver more sermons on the evils of demon rum.

The ultimate example of Baptists and bootleggers, of course, is Prohibition. From 1920 to 1933, the sale of alcohol was against the law in this country, and Americans drank more than ever. Corruption was widespread throughout the government and law enforcement, and organized crime was elevated to a fine art. Segments of the population profited handsomely, and some attained wealth beyond imagining. At the same time, temperance advocates were thrilled to finally live in a society that was morally pure.

From the earliest days of the American republic, the consumption of alcohol could be described as an epidemic. Americans drank morning, noon, and night. There were fourteen thousand distilleries in the country by 1810, and consumption of spirits averaged five gallons per person per year—that's hard liquor, not beer, wine, or cider. Several decades later, estimates of consumption ranged as high as ten or twelve gallons per head. The current figure hovers around one gallon.

By 1830 there were more than one thousand temperance societies scattered around the country. Few observers could argue that the effects of excessive drinking on society were not devastating. Drunkenness led to poverty, wife-beating, loss of wages, disease, and early death. Curiously, though, from the beginning the reformers were only concerned about the effects of alcohol on the lower and working classes. While the country's moneyed and propertied elite drank just as much as their socially inferior brethren, their excesses were not perceived as a problem. Perhaps they should have been, since this was the only group that was legally allowed to vote, and they were also the ones who were governing the country, but no one presumed to tell them how to behave. It was an extension of the social divide that had flourished since the Whiskey Rebellion, when wealthy men such as George Washington could afford to pay the taxes on their stills to further enrich themselves, while small farmers desperate to survive were denied the opportunity to augment their income.

In its earliest days the temperance movement focused on individual abstinence rather than bringing about wholesale revisions in the nation's laws. This had begun to change by the late 1840s, spurred by the conversion of popular figures such as P. T. Barnum to the prohibitionist cause. Barnum was inspired by reformers such as Neal Dow. After being elected mayor of Portland, Maine, in 1851, Dow engineered the first statewide ban on alcohol. Even though the Maine Law was repealed in 1855 after well-publicized riots, it encouraged a dozen other states to pass similar statutes.

The situation alarmed potential whiskey entrepreneurs such as the young Hiram Walker. Walker had moved to Detroit from his native Massachusetts; after amassing a significant amount of seed money from a string of successful businesses, he decided to open a distillery, but was disturbed by the growing anti-alcohol sentiment in America. He crossed the river and set up his new venture in

Windsor, Ontario, which became the home of the whiskey later known as Canadian Club.

Temperance picked up significant momentum after the Civil War, largely because the nation's women adopted the crusade as their own. It was logical for them to do so, since they were

Federal agents pour confiscated whiskey down the drain during Prohibition.
PUBLIC DOMAIN

the ones suffering the most from the drunkenness of their brothers, husbands, and fathers. There was never any shortage of charismatic figures in their ranks. In 1873 a woman named Eliza Thompson, later known as Mother Thompson, began leading groups of women into saloons to pray for the souls of the sinners inside. Surprisingly, the tactic worked; many saloons were closed, and numerous drinkers took abstinence pledges.

Not all the ladies were nonviolent, as evidenced by the curious career of Carry Nation, the hatchet-wielding madwoman of popular culture. Nation lived in Kansas, an officially dry state that was saturated with saloons due to the compliance of corrupt officials. She began participating in peaceful demonstrations in the mode of Mother Thompson, but soon realized that it was a far more effective tactic to simply smash the place to pieces. The saloonkeepers whose establishments were destroyed by her famous hatchet had no recourse, since their bars were illegal, and the police were indulgent with her. Carry Nation died in a mental institution in 1911.

One of the positive outgrowths of the temperance movement was the campaign for women's suffrage. Susan B. Anthony and Elizabeth Cady Stanton began their careers as anti-alcohol advocates, before focusing their efforts on securing the female right to vote. Both were active in the Women's Christian Temperance Union. Founded in 1874, it eventually grew to include 250,000 members, and became one of the most important political action groups in the country. By the end of the century, the WCTU had succeeded in persuading the nation's public schools to institute a curriculum of education on the evils of drinking.

Despite their efforts, consumption of alcohol was not declining. Massive numbers of European immigrants flooded into the United States in the late nineteenth century, and many of them were from beer-producing countries such as Germany. Beer sales went from 36 million gallons in 1850 to 855 million gallons in 1890, and the United States Brewers Association grew into a political force to rival the WCTU. The Brewers Association was dominated by wealthy and successful German-Americans such as Adolphus Busch and Gustave Pabst.

The real architects of Prohibition, however, were Wayne Wheeler and the Anti-Saloon League.

Reverend Howard Hyde Russell established the Anti-Saloon League in Oberlin, Ohio, in 1893 (although he later claimed that it "was begun by Almighty God"). The organization grew rapidly, and was soon the major Prohibitionist group in the country, eclipsing the WCTU. The ASL gave a warm welcome to women, churchgoers, and members of all political parties, but it was not defined by any of those groups. Above all else, it took a practical approach to the challenge of implementing Prohibition: Leaders of the ASL didn't care if politicians drank or not, as long as they voted for the eradication of alcohol sales.

Wayne Wheeler attended Oberlin College and obtained his law degree from Western Reserve University in 1898. He joined the ASL as a field secretary and rose quickly through the ranks, becoming a superintendent in 1902. His key moment occurred in 1906, when he led the fight against the reelection of Ohio Governor Myron T. Herrick. Herrick had refused to go along with

Moonshine Nation

Wayne Wheeler, the brain behind the Anti-Saloon League and the architect of Prohibition. PUBLIC DOMAIN

the ASL's plans to ban alcohol in Ohio, and Wheeler engineered a nasty campaign that squashed him like a bug.

Wheeler became the general counsel and head lobbyist for the national ASL, and conducted one of the shrewdest and most brilliant lobbying efforts in history to enact Prohibition. He ultimately became one of the most influential men in America. "Wayne B. Wheeler," according to his private secretary, Justin Steuart, "controlled six Congresses, dictated to two presidents of the United States, directed legislation in most of the States of the Union, held the balance of power in both Republican and Democratic parties, distributed more patronage than any dozen other men, supervised a federal bureau from outside without official authority, and was recognized by friend and foe alike as the most masterful and powerful single individual in the United States."

Although Wheeler worked behind the scenes, it was impossible for anyone to be elected to Congress—or to successfully hold a House or Senate seat—without supporting the ASL agenda. Once it got started, the ASL juggernaut took on a force of its own and destroyed everything in its path. It was eerily similar to the power of the NRA a century later: Putting aside the merits of the gun-control debate, senators and congressmen could not get elected in certain parts of the country without the support of that organization. Whether or not they truly believed in gun rights was beside the point, as long as they lined up on the right side when the vote was taken.

Still, the ASL faced a fundamental dilemma. Ever since Abraham Lincoln reinstituted the excise tax on whiskey during the Civil War, the proceeds from that tax had accounted for at least one-third of the government's revenues. If the sale of alcohol was outlawed, how would the United States meet its obligations? Despite Wheeler's consummate skills as a lobbyist and political manipulator, the pivotal point in the legalization of Prohibition occurred in 1913 with the passage of the sixteenth amendment to the Constitution: the enactment of the federal income tax. Once the government was assured of an alternative source of operating capital, the path to Prohibition was clear.

In 1917 work began on the eighteenth amendment, which would outlaw the sale of alcoholic beverages. Wheeler and the ASL received an unexpected bonus in the form of America's entry into World War I. Most of the country's breweries were owned by families of German descent, and Wheeler was able to play on the popular sentiment that drinking beer was an unpatriotic act that aided the enemy. He took advantage of the widespread anti-Semitism that still plagued the nation, encouraging publicity that reminded people that the distilling industry was largely controlled by Jewish interests. Even worse was the ASL's exploitation of the country's racial divide. More than half a century after the Civil War, wealthy citizens of most Southern still states lived in fear of their former slaves, and one of the most frightening specters of all was the vision of black men getting drunk and roaming the countryside. "The negro, fairly docile and industrious, becomes, when filled with liquor, turbulent and dangerous and a menace to life, property, and the repose of the community." That quote was from an editorial in the Nashville *Tennessean*—one that ran on the front page, no less. Wheeler fanned the flames of this widespread fear whenever he could.

Early in 1919 the eighteenth amendment was approved by a two-thirds majority of the states; the Volstead Act, which specified criteria for enforcement, was passed separately. The permitted exceptions included sacramental wine, medicinal whiskey prescribed by a physician, and—amazingly—hard cider. At midnight on January 17, 1920, Prohibition took effect and the country went dry. "The nondrinkers had been organizing for fifty years and the drinkers had no organization whatsoever," observed humorist George Ade. "They had been too busy drinking."

Once again the moneyed elite had no need to worry. One of the loopholes in the legislation exempted alcohol that was stored in someone's residence prior to January 16. This allowed wealthy individuals to furnish lavish wine cellars in their numerous homes, as well as purchase hundreds of cases of spirits for future consumption: Not only did they have the necessary cash, but they also had the storage space to accommodate years or decades worth of alcohol. The poor and the working classes would have to shift for themselves, reassured by the knowledge that the government was looking out for their best interests.

Although consumption fell in 1920, as did deaths related to alcoholism, Prohibition was doomed from the start. In the first six months alone, nine hundred thousand cases of whiskey were transferred from various Canadian distilleries to Windsor, the departure point for Detroit. Twenty months after Prohibition began, the Office of the Commissioner of Internal Revenue (forerunner of the IRS) estimated that bootlegging had become a business bringing in more than $1 billion annually. The Prohibition Bureau, the government's enforcement arm, was

Mountain moonshine stills had to be located out of sight and near a source of pure water. PUBLIC DOMAIN.

The stills had to be both isolated and within reach of a road, since everything had to be carried in and out. PUBLIC DOMAIN

underfunded from the start, and initially fielded no more than 1,500 poorly trained agents.

Then there was the problem of bribery and corruption, which was so widespread as to be practically universal. It started at the top. In the fall of 1920, Wayne Wheeler masterminded the election of Warren Harding as the country's twenty-ninth president. Harding was an amiable, vacuous senator from Ohio with no qualifications other than good looks and a talent for back-slapping. He was an outward supporter of Prohibition but benefited from an inexhaustible supply of bootleg liquor, which he served to his cronies at various secret houses. Wheeler controlled him throughout his presidency, which was just as well, since Harding lacked the intellectual capacity to do the job. His administration was quickly taken over by venal Cabinet members, although the details of the worst of the scandals—the so-called "Teapot Dome" affair—only surfaced after his death in 1923.

Between 1920 and 1930, two-thirds of the Prohibition Bureau agents were fired, although in many cases the causes weren't specified. It was possible to find agents who weren't on the bootleggers' payrolls, as we all know from *The Untouchables,* but such men were rare. In places such as Chicago and Detroit, the police department and municipal government were corrupt from top to bottom, and the cities were ruled by crime bosses (Al Capone in Chicago, and the Purple Gang in Detroit). Organized crime had existed before Prohibition, but after 1920 it became the most profitable industry in America, and would never go away.

Back in Windsor the grandsons of Hiram Walker established a subsidiary called United Traders to ship whiskey to destinations around the world; most of it ended up being smuggled back into the United States. By 1925, they were sending one hundred thousand cases of whiskey to Cuba annually. A great deal of the booze shipped by United Traders went to the island of St. Pierre, a French possession off the coast of Newfoundland. The liquor never actually left the ships anchored in port—after the government collected their duty, it was sent directly out again. By the end of Prohibition, the entire population of the island was employed processing liquid cargo.

Once the whiskey left St. Pierre, it headed back to America's Eastern Seaboard, to an area known as Rum Row, located just outside the limit of international waters. There it was unloaded onto "mother ships" and stored until it could be ferried to shore. Bootleggers such as Gertrude Lythgoe and Bill (The Real) McCoy loaded their cargo onto smaller, faster boats and landed at prearranged points along the coast.

A large chunk of the production of Hiram Walker and Sons went directly from Windsor's twenty-two export docks across the river to Detroit (according to Art Jahns, Canadian Club's unofficial historian, one of those docks was controlled by Joseph P. Kennedy, the father of our thirty-fifth president). There was a cable-operated underground submarine capable of holding sixty cases of booze that shuttled back and forth to Grosse Point; in the winter, liquor was simply hauled across the frozen Detroit River. In any case, there was no need to worry: Federal agents in the area didn't have access to a single boat to intercept the shipments.

The fortunes being made by men such as Kennedy were remarkable. In 1923 a case of Canadian Club sold for $7 in Windsor, and was worth $75 in Chicago. Figures like these attracted the attention of Sam Bronfman, a young Canadian who was the son of Moldovan immigrants. Bronfman began his career in the liquor industry shortly after the turn of the century, and Prohibition launched him into hyperspace. By 1922 he was reputed to control a whiskey smuggling ring that brought in nearly $400,000 in profits each month. He traveled to Kentucky and bought the dormant Greenbrier Distillery outside Louisville, transported it to Montreal, and reassembled it piece by piece. Eventually he was able to corner the market on the importation of Scotch whiskey into the United States, most of which was processed through the Bahamas. He reportedly dealt with crime figures such as Meyer Lansky, who chartered his own ships to bring the Scotch safely across the ocean. "By the middle twenties," said Lansky, "we were running the most efficient international shipping business in the world." Bronfman's company, Distillers Corporation Limited, eventually acquired and ran Seagram's. During his later years, when he became the most powerful beverage executive in America, he frequently expressed bafflement over how so much bootleg liquor could have found its way into the country.

Wheeler died in 1927, but the ASL was still able to engineer the defeat of New York Governor Al Smith in the 1928 presidential election by portraying him as both a drinker and an enemy of Prohibition, both of which were true. As the end of the decade approached, the country was tiring of a radical social experiment that had obviously failed, and the wealthy classes were actually expressing solidarity with their poorer counterparts in their desire for repeal. While income tax rates had decreased

Women played an important yet seldom acknowledged role in the creation of illicit whiskey. PUBLIC DOMAIN

during the 1920s, individuals with annual incomes over $50,000 still bore nearly 80 percent of the tax burden. The lightbulb going off over the millionaires' heads illuminated the appealing prospect that the income tax might even be abolished if liquor was legalized and the whiskey tax once again took effect.

Even so, the party might have continued indefinitely without the stock market crash of October 1929. In the Depression that followed, America was once again suffering a fiscal crisis of monumental proportions. The income tax was no longer the answer, since there was very little income left to be taxed. Repeal began to seem more and more certain, and was assured after Roosevelt was elected in 1932. Full-strength beer was legalized in the spring of 1933; on December 5, Prohibition was officially over.

Looking back on it, Prohibition raises many more questions than we can possibly answer. Did the anti-alcohol forces sincerely think that a piece of legislation would eradicate drinking? Apparently they wanted to believe it so badly that they ignored all evidence that it wasn't working. On one level it's hard to fault their good intentions, since alcohol abuse was responsible for many of the social problems of nineteenth-century America. The Prohibitionists went one step further, however, and elevated their cause to the level of a religious crusade. Their theory was an astonishing one in the United States of America: Drinking alcohol violates my religious beliefs, therefore you shouldn't be allowed to drink. If they had taken a break from their efforts to pass the eighteenth amendment and actually read Article I of the Constitution ("Congress shall make no law respecting an establishment of religion"), Prohibition might not have come to pass.

The truth was that nineteenth-century America was not just a Christian nation but an overwhelmingly Protestant one, and very far from the multicultural haven it might seem today. In the latter part of the century, most of the new citizens who arrived in the tidal wave of immigration were Catholic. The ASL was keenly aware how unsettling this was to the country's original settlers. Their propaganda machine, which at its height turned out forty tons of mail each month, characterized the Catholic immigrants as beer-drinking, wine-guzzling heathens controlled from Rome, dedicated to undermining the American way of life. In large part their 1928 campaign to defeat Al Smith succeeded because Smith was a Catholic.

One of the legacies of Prohibition was the creation of a comprehensive federal bureaucracy to administer and collect alcohol taxes. Anyone who has worked in the wine and spirits industry can testify to the thoroughness of the TTB (the Alcohol and Tobacco Tax and Trade Bureau, successor to the ATF). Their detailed and exhaustive procedures are dedicated to making certain that the government receives every cent of tax revenue it is entitled to. Prohibition was an expensive lesson for the feds, and they have no intention of repeating any part of it. After its repeal, a new generation of revenue agents combed the backwoods, intent on arresting moonshiners who were evading the law.

For the most part they didn't succeed, and in many cases their efforts to stem the tidal wave of moonshine were comical. As soon as stills were busted, their contents were simply moved somewhere else. Each new raid reinforced the belief of moonshiners that the government was out to prevent them from making a living and to destroy their way of life. Another unintended consequence of Prohibition was that it vastly expanded the distribution market for illegal liquor. The top-tier figures such as Kennedy and Bronfman may be famous in retrospect, but they were operating on a plane far removed from the average person; even men such as Percy Flowers and George Remus, whose stories we'll examine shortly, were basically CEOs of large regional operations. On the local level the small-time moonshiner suddenly had access to a distribution network to which they would never have otherwise been exposed, and those networks stayed in operation after Prohibition ended.

We all yearn for simple answers to complex questions. Had the God-fearing Prohibitionists listened to their own sermons, they would have realized that evil takes many forms and given the Devil his due. Not only didn't this happen back then, but it hasn't been commonplace since 1933 either. Currently there are eighteen states with Alcohol Beverage Control boards—places where the sale of beer, wine, and liquor is controlled by the state. There are also over 150 counties in the United States that are totally dry, and countless others that have partial restrictions on the sale of alcohol. Not surprisingly, often these are the places that have the most active moonshine cultures. Prohibition was the ultimate duet of the Baptists and bootleggers, and their dance continues.

☆　☆　☆

KING OF THE MOONSHINERS

Do an Internet search for Joshua Percy Flowers (1903–1982), and you'll discover a man who was the proverbial pillar of his community. In this case the community was Clayton, North Carolina, in Johnston County, on the banks of the Neuse River. According to some versions of his biography, he began buying farmland in the area during the Depression and eventually accumulated five thousand acres, on which he grew cotton and tobacco. He has been described as an "avid hunter and outdoorsman" who raised champion walker hounds, and had amassed three hundred of them before his death. He was active in business, civic life, and state and local politics. He was a deacon of his church. He had two children: a son, Percy Jr., who was killed in a private plane crash, and a daughter named Rebecca, who was born in 1950. After his death, Rebecca transformed the bulk of his property into Flowers Plantation, a master planned community filled with upscale residences nestled on sprawling homesites.

Around Johnston County, however, the legend of Percy Flowers is slightly different.

On August 2, 1958, the *Saturday Evening Post* ran a long feature story by John Kobler titled "King of the Moonshiners." According to the piece, North Carolina was the state producing the largest amount of illegal liquor—one-fifth of the national total at the time—and the number-one bootlegger in the state was Percy Flowers. Authorities estimated his annual profit to be in excess of $1 million annually, the equivalent of more than $8 million today.

It seemed like a very strange story for the *Post* to print. This was a magazine almost totally devoted to perpetuating the nostalgic image of a bygone America. Month after month, the famous Norman Rockwell covers depicted adorable puppies, cherubic young boys playing stickball in vacant lots, bountiful Thanksgiving dinners, and Christmas mornings with entire families gathered around the tree. The rest of the content of the August 2 issue was more typical. There was an inspirational piece by Roy Campanella, the Dodgers' catcher who had been paralyzed in an automobile accident and was struggling to walk again, and a charming memoir by actor David Niven that recounted his Hollywood escapades. A photo essay on lower Manhattan's Mulberry Street circa the end of the nineteenth century depicted Italian immigrants who were cheerful, well-fed, and well-scrubbed, rather than living in the crowded and filthy tenements that filled the area at that time.

The *Post* treated Flowers as an American icon, someone who was both admired and feared in his community, a rugged individualist who defied the law with impunity. At times the Kobler piece reads more like a prospective movie treatment than a work of investigative journalism. He dwells on Flowers's fleet of custom-built Cadillacs, the champion walker hound for which he paid $15,000, and the thousands he regularly wagered on illegal cockfights. Basically the *Post* took a notorious regional figure and elevated him to the status of a national hero. They described his philanthropic activities and his active participation in the White Oaks Baptist Church, where his wife, Delma, taught Sunday school. According to the reverend, "Both Mr. and Mrs. Flowers have helped more people than any couple I know of." "He's easy to get along with, most agreeable," said Charles M. Johnson, one of Flowers's foxhunting buddies who ran unsuccessfully for governor in 1948. "I never went on a trip with a better-behaved man." Juxtaposed against that, however, was the portrait of someone who used brutal tactics to control a vast illegal empire. "In his behalf," wrote Kobler, "his loyal followers have been known to knife and shoot up their own kin." Flowers, Kobler said, was "courtly of manner when deferred to, violent when thwarted, and rules his domain with a baronial hand."

Between 1929 and 1958, Flowers was the subject of ten federal and eighteen state or local indictments. The charges included everything from operating a slot machine and unlawful possession of a pistol to bootlegging, income- and liquor-tax evasion, and assault with intent to kill. He managed to evade them all, although when the *Post* story appeared he had finally been sent to prison for one year on a contempt charge—for threatening a federal revenue agent who was testifying against him during a liquor-tax trial. The judge who sentenced him was apologetic, extolling Flowers as a good man who just hadn't been able to perceive that "the law is a little bigger than he is."

The judge may have had it backwards. In Johnston County the law appeared to be pretty much whatever Percy Flowers said it was (in 1936, according to Kobler, Jimmy and Dick Flowers—Percy's brothers—intercepted federal agent Elliott Bennett, who was snooping around the farm; the two men pistol-whipped the agent and nearly killed him). The heart of his operation was a general store located on Highway 42 outside Clayton. Groceries and assorted household supplies were sold there, while moonshine was dispensed to known customers from the back of the house. Those drive-up transactions were as close as Percy Flowers ever got to the sale of illegal alcohol. His enormous stills, capable of churning out thousands of gallons of hooch, were located on parcels of his property farmed by sharecroppers. When local talent proved insufficient to manage the production, he imported two master distillers from the Great Smoky Mountains. The bootleg liquor was transported to market by a tight circle of skilled drivers.

Flowers paid his people well, and inspired absolute loyalty in return. In 1955 an employee named Signal Wall shot his brother Weldon for "talking too much." He then knifed and blackjacked another brother, Macon, and left the man in a ditch. Wall got twelve years at hard labor. After he escaped from a chain gang he remained free for six months, even though his hiding places were known to Johnston County authorities. It was widely rumored that

Percy Flowers had arranged for his escape. When Wall was finally apprehended by state investigators, he was living in a cottage on Flowers's farm.

Kobler's story in the *Saturday Evening Post* cemented the legend of Percy Flowers in the American imagination. That legend was further embellished by documentaries such as *Mr. Percy's Run*, an independent video made by D. L. Anderson years after Flowers's death. The format of Anderson's brief documentary consists of segments about foxhunting and Flowers's passionate involvement in it, interspersed with reminiscences about the Moonshine King from people who knew him. Banjo music floats in and out of the background, and the general tenor of the film is both romantic and reverential.

"Percy Flowers was one of the smartest human beings I ever met," says Richie Creech, son of a driver who hauled moonshine for Flowers and grandson of "Sugar Daddy" Boykin, one of the men who operated the stills. "He was going to be successful at whatever he did. You didn't want to match wits with Percy Flowers."

"I asked him one day," says a voice off camera, "Percy, they tell me that you made and sold a bunch of whiskey."

"Made it, or had it made?" was the response. "Sold it, or had it sold?"

The local attitudes toward him were best summed up by the *Raleigh Times,* right after he went to jail for contempt in 1958, in comments that—depending on your perspective—could either be construed as critical or full of admiration: "Flowers, with his big cars, his expensive cattle, his hunting dogs, and his benefactions to the needy and the church, is a sort of Robin Hood to the small fry which make up the bulk of our criminal population. They bask in the reflected glory every time he makes a monkey out of the law."

Perry Sullivan, in a book titled *Lost Flowers*, gives us a totally different picture of the Moonshine King. The author paints a sympathetic portrait of Flowers as a man of his word, someone who was loyal and compassionate toward his employees, and above all a loving and devoted parent. On the last claim, Sullivan should know: He was one of two illegitimate children fathered by Percy Flowers.

His story is a remarkable one. Willis "Curry" Sullivan managed Percy's general store on Highway 42. Curry and his wife, Beatrice, had been trying unsuccessfully to have children for a number of years. Beatrice began an illicit affair with Percy Flowers, and Perry was born in May 1962; a daughter followed several years later. "I was born out of a married woman's yearning to have children and the king's willingness to fulfill her need," Sullivan writes. He likens the relationship to a modern-day *droit de seigneur*, a French medieval custom wherein the king had the first claim on the wombs of his peasants' female relations—although in those days the king tended to be more interested in the virgin daughters of his peasants rather than their wives.

Even more dramatic was the message that Percy Flowers delivered to Curry Sullivan shortly after the birth of his son. According to a longtime employee named Howard (or Reno, as he was called), who had worked in Flowers's liquor operation since the 1920s, Percy took Curry aside one day during Bea's pregnancy and informed Curry that the child was his. "You won't ever say a thang, not one word, to Bea about it," he informed Curry within earshot of Reno. "If you can't live with it, then it will be your ass that has to go."

Curry lived with it for the rest of his life, managing the store and tending the foxhounds, working fourteen and fifteen hours each day, six days each week. Perry rarely saw him during his childhood, and later observed that his life must have been full of "fear and hatred." Percy Flowers, on the other hand, drove out to the house every day (a house that he also owned) in one of his Cadillacs. He doted over Perry and his sister, Tammy, and was an exceptional father in every respect. He made no secret of the fact that the two children were his, and gave them everything possible—except his last name, of course. Percy and Perry were extremely close. By the 1960s the Flowers moonshine empire had shrunken dramatically, and Percy had more time on his hands. Perry spent most of his childhood days at the store, except for the occasions when he was out foxhunting or attending cockfights with Percy. Sunday mornings were occupied by the Pentecostal Church, and summers were spent working in Percy's tobacco fields.

As difficult as the situation must have been for Curry Sullivan, it was also agonizing for Percy's wife, Delma, and their two children. The Flowers family lived across the street from the general store, and from her bedroom window she had to watch Percy coming and going every day with Perry in tow. Delma Flowers had spent most of her life earning a well-deserved reputation as a leader in her church and community, only to see it undone by the shame of

Perry and Tammy. That shame may be hard to understand fifty years later, living in a society where alternative behaviors are more accepted, but things were very different in the conservative and closed culture of the rural South in the 1960s. Illegitimate children certainly existed, but just as surely you didn't brag about them.

Perry Sullivan's teenage rebellion took the form of a brief interval away from home, during which he became a champion motocross racer. By the time he returned to Johnston County in the late 1970s, he decided to follow in his father's footsteps and make moonshine. At first, an aging and ailing Percy tried to dissuade him, but he finally relented and allowed Reno to educate his son in the trade. They set up a still near a natural spring on Percy's property, and Perry learned his father's recipe for moonshine. He did make some money from it, even though the glory days of large-scale production were over.

Perry Sullivan's moonshine career was cut short by Percy's death in 1982. The local sheriff warned him to leave the liquor business alone, since with Percy gone there was nothing he could do for Perry if the law caught him. Sullivan had to cope with the dual tragedies of losing his father, along with the emotional and financial security his father had given him. Percy's wife and surviving daughter, Rebecca, weren't keen on acknowledging the existence of two illegitimate children and made no provisions for the Sullivans as Percy's assets were gradually sold off. The family was forced to move out of their house, and struggled to survive for several years.

Gradually, Perry Sullivan rallied. He took flying lessons and resolved to join the service as a pilot, but that required a college degree. He got accepted at East Carolina University and worked his way through school, where he joined the ROTC. After college he flew fighter jets for the air force and eventually became a commercial airline pilot.

Lost Flowers is written as an epistle to Perry's two sons, in the hope that they would finally know their own heritage. It is lyrical and nostalgic without being self-conscious, and provides a detailed look at life in the Appalachian South, as well as the hard work of operating a moonshine still. He is full of sincere compassion for Curry, for his mother and sister, and particularly for Delma and Rebecca Flowers, referring to all of them as victims of the situation. Even though Rebecca hasn't maintained an adult relationship with him, he is sensitive to the impact the moonshine operation must have had on her as a young girl, not to mention witnessing her mother's constant discomfort and shame over the existence of her half-brother and sister. He admires her accomplishment in transforming the site of Percy's former moonshine empire into Flowers Plantation, and recognizes that her hard work and persistence are traceable to "ole Percy's DNA"—genetics that, at the end of the day, they still share.

Rebecca Flowers declined to be interviewed for this book, and I suspect that her perspective would have been truly fascinating. On the Flowers Plantation website, Percy is identified simply as someone who owned the property from the 1920s to 1982, and "whose family today works to preserve the area's traditions and historical roots." Those roots are not specified, and there is no mention of moonshine.

The community offers families "gracious living in beautiful, natural settings away from urban noise and congestion." In late 2013, home listings ranged from $155,000 to $375,000. There are walking and biking trails, a large fitness center, and a clubhouse with a spa and cafe. Three golf courses are nearby. Ironically, very close to the spot where federal agent Elliott Bennett was pistol-whipped in 1936, the newest generation of North Carolina matrons can indulge in facials, manicures, and permanents.

☆ ☆ ☆

BOOTLEGGING, INC.

On the morning of October 6, 1927, a man named George Remus was on his way to his divorce hearing in Cincinnati. His chauffeur-driven car had been following a taxi containing two female passengers—his wife, Imogene, and his adopted daughter, Ruth. At his direction, the driver forced the taxi off the road in Eden Park. Most accounts are consistent on what happened next: Imogene escaped from the cab; Remus hunted her down and shot her once in the stomach at close range. She was rushed to a nearby hospital where she was pronounced dead. Remus went to the police station and cheerfully turned himself in.

George Remus is not well known today, but during the 1920s he was one of the most successful businessmen in America. In his best year, his organization reputedly made close to $100 million, or the equivalent of nearly $1.5 billion in today's money. Remus, however, was not the head of US Steel or General Motors. He was a captain of industry, but his industry was bootlegging.

Remus was born in Germany in November 1874, but grew up in Chicago. He was ambitious from an early age. When his father was incapacitated in 1890, he took on the responsibility of supporting his family and went to work in his uncle's drugstore. He attended the Chicago College of Pharmacy and obtained a pharmacist's license at nineteen, after lying about his age. He bought the drugstore from his uncle in 1895 and soon owned a second one.

Not content to be a pharmacist, he went to law school at night and was admitted to the Illinois bar at age twenty-six. He set up practice as a defense attorney, and—in an omen of things to come—specialized in murder cases, particularly controversial and lurid ones.

He was catapulted to national prominence in 1914 with his defense of William Cheney Ellis, a Cincinnati leather merchant who had killed his wife in a Chicago hotel room. Remus decided to argue temporary insanity, which he described as "transitory insanity"; he was one of the first attorneys in the country to do so. The trial generated huge amounts of publicity, and Remus provided a succession of expert witnesses who testified that the defendant had not known right from wrong and was therefore not responsible for his actions. Ellis was found guilty and sentenced to fifteen years; Remus regarded this as a victory, since his client had escaped the gallows. In light of future events, the most prophetic moment came during Remus's closing, when he informed the jury, "William Cheney Ellis was insane when he killed the woman he loved better than any other in the world."

As Prohibition approached, and particularly within the transitional period between the passage of the Volstead Act in January 1919 and the abolition of liquor sales in January 1920,

Remus defended more bootlegging clients. Prolonged exposure to these defendants demonstrated two things to him. On one hand, they were fabulously wealthy; at the same time, most were of limited intelligence. He speculated on exactly how wealthy a man with considerable brains—someone like himself—could become if he applied himself to the task of supplying bootleg liquor. He began searching for a loophole in the law.

What he initially stumbled on was the provision in the Volstead Act that exempted inventories of alcohol sitting in private residences or warehouses when Prohibition took effect. This was no small amount of booze. As of January 1920 some two hundred million gallons of liquor were stored in the nation's 503 distilleries. The problem, of course, was how to legally get the booze out of the warehouses and sell it to the public. He found the solution in another loophole that allowed citizens to buy liquor for medicinal purposes, if armed with a doctor's prescription. This was already becoming an industry unto itself, as tens of thousands of physicians were writing prescriptions to supplement their income. Remus devised a system where he would function as a middleman, withdrawing the whiskey from warehouses with legitimate government permits and using drug companies to sell the product to pharmacies, where it could then be dispensed.

He wasn't able to do this in Chicago, however, where Johnny Torrio and Al Capone were moving in on the bootlegging business with the collusion of City Hall and the police department. He moved to Cincinnati, where 80 percent of the nation's bonded whiskey was stored within three hundred miles of the city. Before relocating he married his second wife, Imogene, and adopted her daughter Ruth.

Once in Cincinnati, Remus purchased two wholesale drug companies; he also bought a distillery. He located his family on a ten-acre estate in the suburb of Price Hill and went to work. By 1921 he controlled an empire, employing three thousand people and using a fleet of 150 trucks to ferry liquor to nine states. He bought a fifty-acre estate outside the city called Death Valley Farm, which served as a depot for the shipments. By the end of the year he owned nine distilleries. Remus closed out 1921 by throwing a party to celebrate the installation of a $100,000 swimming pool at Price Hill. The pool was surrounded by a Roman garden and conservatory. As the clock neared midnight, he distributed diamond stickpins and earrings as party favors to more than one hundred guests.

The success of Remus's scheme earned him many enemies. The most obvious ones were bosses of organized crime such as Meyer Lansky, Chicago's Johnny Torrio, and Detroit's Purple Gang. Initially the government seemed to be the least of his problems. Corruption was widespread during the administration of President Warren G. Harding, and Remus conscientiously paid off everyone he could find in the Justice Department and the upper echelons of the Prohibition Bureau. Unfortunately for him, the one official beyond his reach was Assistant Attorney General Mabel Willebrandt, an early feminist crusader who campaigned feverishly for the enforcement of Prohibition and earned the nickname "First Lady of the Law."

Death Valley Farm was raided toward the end of 1921; there were vast amounts of liquor moving in and out of the facility, and the government was able to prove that not all of it was covered by legitimate permits. Remus was facing possible indictment, but he was not worried. He had paid more than $250,000 to Jess Smith, the confidant of Attorney General Harry Daugherty. Smith assured him that even if he went to trial, the Justice Department would ensure he would never be convicted. Smith was wrong. Remus was tried in April 1922, convicted of violating the Volstead Act, and sentenced to two years in prison. Shortly afterward Jess Smith committed suicide, voiding Remus's federal insurance policy. As his case progressed through the appeals courts it was business as usual for Remus, who continued to consolidate his empire and even bought a controlling interest in Jack Daniel's. Mabel Willebrandt pursued him ruthlessly and tirelessly, as she would throughout the 1920s. She had heard the rumors that he would never serve a day in jail. After Harding's death she brought the Remus case to the attention of the new president, Calvin Coolidge, and monitored its progress throughout the appeals process. By early 1924 Remus had run out of options. Before leaving for prison, he gave Imogene power of attorney over all his assets.

He was transferred to Atlanta Federal Penitentiary and given a cell on "Millionaire's Row." Initially he was assigned a soft job in the library, and ate his meals apart from the other prisoners. These privileges soon dried up under pressure from the government, however, and Remus was desperate to get out of jail. He wrote to Imogene in Cincinnati and suggested that she contact an investigator for the Prohibition Bureau named Franklin Dodge, who fellow inmates said had an inside track within the Justice Department.

It turned out to be the wrong move. Imogene became infatuated with Dodge and began an affair with him. Before long the two were conspiring to have Remus deported on charges that he had never been naturalized as a US citizen. Imogene began liquidating his assets and hiding the money, and eventually filed for divorce.

Remus was released from prison in September 1925. Facing a long list of other indictments, he became a federal witness and received a grant of immunity. Even so, he returned to prison in 1926 to serve a one-year sentence on a previous conviction, and Imogene renewed her efforts to get him deported. He was released for good in April 1927 and headed for the mansion at Price Hill. He was shocked by what he saw. The windows had been nailed shut, and his clothes were piled up at the back door. Remus and a friend broke into the house and discovered that it had been stripped clean.

This incident pushed Remus into a complete emotional breakdown. His divorce case proceeded, but progress was slowed down due to his mental state. Finally a date was set for a hearing on Thursday, October 27, 1927, the morning he hunted Imogene down and killed her.

After the shooting, Remus took a cab to the police station and surrendered (his chauffeured car had fled the scene as events unfolded). When informed of his wife's death, he said: "She who dances down the primrose path must die on the primrose path. I'm happy. This is the first peace of mind I've had in two years."

The Imogene Remus murder was national news, and Remus was once again a celebrity. On the night of the shooting, he even held a press conference in his cell. He cheerfully continued to take responsibility for the crime, although he implied that he might have been temporarily deranged when he pulled the trigger. When he was arraigned for the murder, he pled not guilty.

The prosecution of George Remus for the murder of his wife may not have been the trial of the century, but it was near the top of the charts. By the time the proceedings started in the fall of 1927, most of the country had already come to view Prohibition as a silly and failed exercise in nationally imposed morality. The Remus case, though, contained all the basic elements for a thriller: sex, infidelity, bootlegging, and murder. On top of that, the trial occurred in a media environment void of TV and the Internet, making it one of the prime focuses of national entertainment.

Remus acted as his own counsel, backed up by prominent Cincinnati defense attorney Charles Elston. The lead prosecutor was Charles P. Taft II, son of Supreme Court chief justice and former president William Howard Taft. In an echo of his 1914 defense of William Cheney Ellis, Remus based his case on temporary insanity. Hostilities erupted during jury selection, as Taft objected that an insane man should not be allowed to examine prospective jurors. Remus and Elston managed to convince the judge that insanity was only being alleged for the moment of the murder, and the objection was overruled.

The prosecution completely botched the case, much as it would seven decades later in the O. J. Simpson criminal trial. Witness after witness evoked sympathy for Remus, and offered the opinion that the ordeal he had been subjected to by Imogene was sufficient to provoke insanity. On December 20 the jury deliberated for nineteen minutes and found Remus not guilty. He was confined briefly in a mental institution, and finally freed for good in January 1928.

Remus never returned to bootlegging, and in any case the industry had changed. By the late 1920s the transport and sale of illegal liquor had become the sole province of organized crime, and it was a dangerous game in which Remus would have been completely overmatched. He had been lucky enough to hit the window of opportunity immediately after the passage of Prohibition, before the traffic in illegal booze became highly criminalized. He tried his hand at a number of businesses, all of which failed, and he finally concentrated his efforts on an unsuccessful legal battle to recover part of his lost empire. He died in 1952.

The story of George Remus is a distinctly American tale. Most writers who have chronicled his life depict his rise and fall as a saga of pure greed, and that may be so. He was certainly motivated by a burning desire for status, and in fact almost penetrated the upper reaches of Cincinnati social life. Just as certainly, it had little to do with liquor or the right of individuals to consume it. Ironically, Remus was a teetotaler, and the King of the Bootleggers never tasted alcohol once in his life.

HEADS, TAILS, AND HEARTS

Wine is a product of nature. If you take a bunch of grapes, crush them and bring the juice to the right temperature, wild yeasts on the surface of the skins will convert the grape sugars to alcohol. No one knows for sure when it was first produced, but there's evidence to suggest that wine goes back around eight thousand years. It's likely that the first batch was made by accident. We can even picture the scene: Workers carry heavy loads of grapes in from the fields at harvest time; the grapes on the bottom are crushed by the weight of the fruit on top; fermentation begins spontaneously in the late summer heat; someone drinks the potion, likes it, and a craze is born.

Liquor, on the other hand, had to be invented, and its existence was far from a foregone conclusion. We can look at grapes and visualize that some sort of beverage might come from them—they do have juice, after all. It takes an overactive imagination to glance at a bushel of wheat, rye, or corn and imagine a jug of whiskey.

We know that the first scientists to work on the process of distillation, in the Egyptian city of Alexandria in the first century AD, were not looking for a short path to intoxication. Those researchers were alchemists, men who were obsessed with finding a method of transforming base metals into gold. As a consolation prize, they would have settled for the elixir of life, the potion that would enable them to live forever. It's understandable that the end product of their experiments would eventually be known as spirits: The procedure that turned grains into alcohol was so bizarre that it seemed mystical and otherworldly.

The first recorded use of distillation to produce potent alcohol occurred in the twelfth century at the School of Salerno, the leading medical facility of the period, located in southern Italy. Presumably the faculty was not concerned with alchemy but instead focused on the creation of patent medicines that could be reproduced throughout Europe. There's evidence that distilled alcohol was being made in China around the same time. An interesting variation called the Mongolian still accomplished the same goal through freeze distillation—by freezing the water out of wine, they were able to easily raise the alcohol level of the beverage.

Mongolians aside, the process of distillation has remained remarkably similar for the past nine hundred years. The theory is simple. Alcohol boils at a lower temperature than water, so the vapor can be isolated; once collected, it can be condensed back into a liquid again. Thus, a fermented beverage with a moderate alcohol level, such as wine, can be transformed into a more concentrated drink. The distiller who wants to take grains or corn and change them into alcohol faces an extra step: He or she must first take the starchy substances and turn them into sugars, so that yeast may start the process of fermentation. This is accomplished by steeping the grains or corn in hot water to create something called a mash.

It sounds simple, but there are challenges and dangers involved. Methanol (otherwise known as methyl alcohol, or wood alcohol) boils at 148 degrees Fahrenheit, while ethanol (ethyl alcohol) boils at 173 degrees. Methanol is extremely toxic, and consumption can cause blindness or death—thus, it's essential for the distiller to find a way to separate it from ethyl alcohol, which is relatively safe to consume in limited quantities.

The classic vessel for all these procedures was (and is) the copper pot still. In the realm of cooking implements, copper is highly prized because of its ability to conduct heat evenly. For this reason the copper pot still has long been a favorite of distillers, provided they could afford one. Several years ago while traveling in Kentucky, I paid a visit to the Vendome Copper and Brass Works in Louisville. Established in 1903, Vendome is the last major still manufacturer left in the country. Before Prohibition they primarily built stills for farmers—equipment that was doubtless used to concoct moonshine—but today most of their business comes from the booming craft distilling market, with the occasional commission from one of Kentucky's major bourbon producers (on their website, they're careful to point out that only the holders of appropriate federal licenses may purchase their handiwork). The vision of those gleaming copper stills, some of which stand several stories high, is a sight most people aren't likely to forget.

Regardless of size, most stills basically function in the same way. As the mash boils in the pot, alcohol vapors are released.

Those vapors travel through a condensing tube designed to cool them, are returned to liquid form, and are collected in another vessel. The result of the first run through the still is referred to as low wine and has an alcohol content of about 20 to 30 percent; it must be distilled at least once more to obtain a full-strength spirit.

At this point the potential dangers come into play, and the distiller's skill becomes important. The first liquor to emerge from the still is referred to as the foreshots or heads, and it will be high in toxic methanol as well as other volatile components. Conversely, the end of the run (referred to as the tails) is generally lower in alcohol and will make the spirit taste flabby and diluted if included. The art of distillation is largely about knowing when to make the cuts between the foreshots and tails to leave the best part of the distillate, known as the heart. The foreshots and tails also contain alcohol esters, which are the product of a reaction between an acid and an alcohol—substances such as fusel oils, proteins, and pectins. Esters aren't necessarily harmful, and including some in the final blend is a good way to add complexity to the spirit. They are roughly analogous to tars and nicotine in tobacco. You can engineer a cigarette that has most of the impurities removed; it will be healthier, but it will also lack taste.

Distillation was revolutionized with the invention of the continuous still, patented by Irishman Aeneas Coffey in 1830. Aside from allowing much larger batches of liquor to be produced at once, the Coffey still had numerous advantages. It enabled distillers to make a cleaner and smoother spirit, one in which the amount of impurities could be controlled and kept to a minimum. The continuous still became enormously popular around the world and is still favored for the mass-production of many quality spirits, although it is illegal in certain areas (such as Cognac, France) where traditional methods are regarded as an essential part of the end product. The recent advent of craft distilling has brought the pot still back into favor.

The pot still had one other significant disadvantage: In the wrong hands, it tended to blow up. Alcohol is extremely flammable when heated to the right temperature and exposed to an ignition source. This isn't much of a worry with table wine, but 40 percent alcohol (or 80 proof, the content of many commercial spirits) has a flash point of 174.2 degrees; for a neutral grain spirit of 90 percent alcohol, the threshold lowers to 145.4 degrees. The history of distillation is filled with such accidents, and they've continued into the present day. In 2011 a massive illegal still ignited in an industrial area outside of Boston, killing five people; the explosion was audible at a distance of five miles, and many witnesses thought the world was coming to an end.

Most moonshine stills were far more modest than the gleaming copper masterpieces turned out by Vendome. They were usually constructed from the materials at hand on the farm, and located near a water source such as a river or spring. Most were quite simple: The vapor traveled through a device known as a lyne arm into the condenser; the condensing coils were housed in a cooling chamber insulated with cold water. The reflux still, popular with moonshiners, also contained a column packed with inert material that led to the lyne arm.

In the popular imagination—and in fact—most moonshine was corn whiskey. There were obviously no formal federal standards regulating the ingredients that went into backyard hooch, but those standards wouldn't have mattered much to moonshiners in any case. Corn was the common cash crop in the South, and the one that was easiest to grow. Most recipes contained between 50 and 100 percent corn; sugar was optional, although some variations (including the moonshine made by mobster Dutch Schultz, currently being revived by Dutch's Spirits in upstate New York) were made from a mash containing nothing but sugar and water.

Much has been written about the health hazards of drinking moonshine, and a great deal of it is likely true. Most shine was made by poor farmers desperate to scratch out a living, and parts for the still were scarce. A common practice was to substitute used automobile or truck radiators for the condenser coils, which increased the likelihood of contamination with ethylene glycol, or antifreeze. While antifreeze has a sweet taste that will improve the flavor profile of shine, it is also poisonous. Another common hazard was lead poisoning. As late as 2006, a study of illegal moonshine samples conducted by a physician at the University of Virginia revealed that forty-three out of forty-eight samples had potentially hazardous or fatal levels of lead. Unscrupulous moonshiners were known to add methanol to their product to boost alcohol levels, not to mention substances such as paint thinner or formaldehyde.

At the end of the day, a great deal depended on knowing your supplier, who ideally was the same person who made the shine. This was entirely possible in the early days of the American republic, and it is still feasible in rural areas today. As the country became more developed, however, the bootlegger supplying the

WARNING

DEADLY POISON
Moonshine Liquor®
Being Distributed Locally

DO NOT DRINK ANY Type of BOOTLEG LIQUOR regardless of source. **DEADLY POISONOUS** Lead Salts are being found in WHITE LIQUOR. This poison can cause **DEATH** or serious illness as much as a year after drinking.

The next SMALL DRINK May Bring the amount of Lead Salts in the Body to the concentration point necessary to cause **DEATH!**

REPORT MOONSHINE STILLS   DURHAM COUNTY ABC LAW ENFORCEMENT   *PHONE: 688-7261*
PHONE:

Poster warning citizens of the dangers of moonshine, many of which were not imaginary. PUBLIC DOMAIN

liquor wasn't necessarily the same person who made it. The density of bars increased as cities grew throughout the South, and sometimes they weren't fussy about who they bought their product from.

How much did moonshine cost? Most accounts seem to peg the price in the range of $25 to $30 per gallon in modern dollars, or the equivalent of $5 to $6 for today's standard 750-milliliter bottle. This is certainly inexpensive when compared to many of the designer vodkas on the market, but remember that moonshine, like vodka, doesn't need to be aged in expensive oak barrels for years. When I first interviewed legendary bootlegger and NASCAR driver Junior Johnson in 2011, he told me that in the 1940s the government wanted to charge $11 for a gallon of whiskey the moonshiners were selling for $3. The unpaid taxes accounted for some of the savings to the consumer, but a large chunk of it could be chalked up to the avoidance of middleman profit—distributor salespeople with company cars and expense accounts, retail liquor stores with multiple employees that take out weekly full-page ads in the local newspaper, etc. The general rule was (and is) that illegal moonshine costs roughly half the price of commercial, taxed liquor.

At the beginning of the twenty-first century, many people began calling for the manufacture of legal moonshine, just as they are calling for the legalization of marijuana in 2014. The moonshine advocates were supported by clusters of municipal governments across the country, not to mention the feds, who realized that they had been cheated out of tax revenue for decades, if not for centuries—revenue that might be earmarked for paving roads, building schools and hospitals, caring for their neediest citizens, and lining the pockets of their most corrupt officials. Starting in 2010 the state governments of the South began falling like dominoes, as steadily as they seceded from the Union 150 years earlier, and moonshine was legalized in many states (and not just Southern states, either).

The remaining question, of course, is whether legally produced moonshine is actually moonshine. The issue is complicated. There are Federal Standards of Identity for whiskey, gin, vodka, brandy, scotch, and virtually every other type of liquor, but not for moonshine. Later in this book I profile a number of legal producers of moonshine, and the criteria for selection was rigorous. Producers of "white whiskey" were excluded. Major bourbon distillers who claimed to bottle "moonshine," such as Buffalo Trace or Heaven Hill, were eliminated as well. While they are certainly turning out a fine product, the distillate is nothing more than the "white dog" that emerges from the still before it goes into charred white oak barrels to become bourbon. There was yet another category of "moonshine" producers who were excluded: serial entrepreneurs who made their fortune elsewhere and thought it would be a neat idea to produce legal moonshine.

This left me with a unique group of people, men who were descended from moonshiners and decided to take up the mantle of generations of their family. Their decision was spurred in part because they didn't have to risk going to prison to make moonshine, but mostly because they were able to pay homage to a trail of courageous people who had preceded them. For them, shine was a mission as much as a product.

In the modern era, moonshine is chic. It has been taken up by the new generation of mixologists, men and women who constantly comb the outer frontiers of the cocktail culture in search of taste sensations that are unique and different. Among home hobbyists, it's all the rage as well. Go online and do an Internet search for "moonshine stills for sale," and you'll come up with hundreds—if not thousands—of results. In addition to stills, many of these sites sell accessories, fittings, yeast, hoses, copper piping, and everything else you might need to successfully make moonshine at home. They'll put you in business for no more than a few hundred dollars. Most are circumspect in their warnings to customers to check out their local and federal laws before firing up their stills, and virtually all of them inform potential moonshiners that they are not allowed to sell the fruits of their labors on the open market without a license. Even so, one site claims that distilling high-quality spirits is "as easy as making coffee," and promises complete training and one-on-one phone support.

In the meantime, are there still thousands of illegal moonshiners up in the hills, making and selling homemade hooch outside the supervision of the authorities?

You betcha.

☆ ☆ ☆

MOONSHINE AND THE LAW

In the popular imagination, the federal revenue agent has the moonshiner in hot pursuit. They weave in and out of corkscrewed country roads at speeds in excess of one hundred miles per hour, until the law overtakes them or one of the cars crashes.

This stereotype was sometimes true, but not very often. To begin with, not all moonshiners could afford fast cars. They certainly had them in places like Wilkes County, North Carolina, where a handful of moonshiners made enough money to afford them, and they did in fact give birth to NASCAR. Remember, though, that the average person who made or hauled moonshine was a poor farmer locked in a desperate struggle to survive; their cars were as serviceable as their income levels, but they generally weren't hot rods. In places such as the Land Between the Lakes, in Kentucky, their cars were likely to be personal vehicles with as many homemade modifications as they could afford.

Most of the revenue men didn't have fast cars either, unless they captured one in a chase—which rarely happened. The typical rural moonshine bust consisted of agents closing in on a still, usually with the help of an informant. Most of the time the still was abandoned by the time the agents found it, due to a crude but effective warning system in which lookouts relayed the news that the revenuers were coming. Moonshiners who got word that they were about to be busted would take the essential and expensive copper parts of their still with them and simply set up somewhere else. When the agents arrived, they destroyed what was left of the still, either by chopping it up or dynamiting it, and chalked up the raid to a triumph of American justice.

On the occasions when the revenue men did capture a modified moonshine car, they usually lacked the skill to drive it. Nor did they have the desire to maneuver the vehicle at speeds of 110 or 120 mph along winding mountain roads as they pursued their prey. As Junior Johnson observed to me, the bootleggers were willing to take all sorts of chances to avoid jail, but the agents had no incentive to risk their necks in the line of duty. It was a job for them, and a secure one, particularly during the Depression. It's difficult to quantify how many people did get killed over the years, although we can assume that more bootleggers than agents perished in the middle of the night. When a revenue man did get killed, he was probably in the wrong place at the wrong moment.

If someone was caught making or hauling moonshine, the actual sentences were relatively light. In Kentucky the standard was a year and a day, and the offender typically served nine months. In North Carolina the sentence averaged two years, and those convicted served between one-third and one-half of that time before they were paroled. One of the ironies of the situation, of course, was that the moonshiners and bootleggers who went to federal prison ended up, in effect, attending school. They had the chance to spend time with their colleagues, and they swapped information and techniques. The average moonshiner emerged from prison much better versed in the art of constructing and operating stills.

In recent years the theory of the penal system has shifted from rehabilitation to punishment. If a prisoner isn't a career criminal when he or she goes in, the odds are they're going to emerge that way. Fifty or sixty years ago the concept was different: Incarceration was viewed as an opportunity for society to redeem a wayward individual. Even so, most moonshiners and bootleggers came out of the penal system with no more ability to earn a living than they went in with, and they almost always reentered a rural society with no jobs or economic opportunity of any sort. The only way they could feed their families was to go back into the business.

Virtually every book I read, and everyone I spoke to on the subject, stressed the imbalance and misdirection of the government's efforts to stamp out moonshine. Down through the centuries of taxation and resistance, crime and punishment, it never seemed to occur to anyone to do anything to improve economic conditions in the Appalachian hills. While the authorities appropriated huge amounts of money to chase down and incarcerate offenders, no roads were built, no skills were taught, and no incentives were given to companies to come to rural areas and provide jobs. In areas where moonshining mostly died out over time, such as Wilkes County, North Carolina, it was the result of industries coming into the area that built plants and hired people. Almost always, when rural residents were given the opportunity to make an honest living, they pounced on it.

One thing I wondered about—and one question I asked, everywhere I went—was whether the revenue men were upstanding public servants, or if they were susceptible to bribes. The answers I received varied considerably. Junior Johnson told me that the agents wouldn't take bribes in Wilkes County, and that judges tended to give harsher sentences to moonshiners and bootleggers who attempted to influence them. In Kentucky, David Balentine wryly observed that the revenue men didn't have the common sense and/or intelligence to take a bribe.

Of course, we know that the reality was very different in many other places. Between 1920 and 1933 the corruption of the Prohibition Bureau agents was widespread and well-documented. There was simply too much illegal money involved, and most of it was difficult to trace. In Johnston County, North Carolina, Percy Flowers had virtually every public official and law enforcement officer in the state paid off, from the governor on down. As a result he was able to operate freely on a large scale, and reportedly brought in train carloads of sugar to fuel his operation. George Remus did the same thing on a national level. He came to believe that he was invulnerable because he had paid more than $250,000 to Jess Smith, the confidant of Attorney General Harry Daugherty. Smith committed suicide in 1923, which left Remus without federal protection and exposed him to prosecution by the

Justice Department. Had that not happened, Remus would likely have gone on to become the richest and most influential man in America.

Most of the payoffs and bribes that did occur conformed to a sad and familiar pattern. It was the little guy at the bottom of the food chain—the moonshiner struggling to put food on the table—who got squeezed badly, while corrupt local officials reaped huge profits. After paying off the law to look the other way, the typical moonshiner was no closer to economic prosperity than he had been when he started his run.

While corruption among law enforcement was endemic during and right after Prohibition, it probably reached its height in Franklin County, Virginia, the setting of the movie *Lawless*. Franklin County was the self-styled "moonshine capital of the world," and may have had a right to claim that title due to the sheer volume of illegal liquor produced there—virtually every citizen in the county was involved one way or another in the production. Authorities estimated that between 1930 and 1935, the quantity of moonshine made there would have generated over $5 million in federal revenue if the stills had been registered (about $87 million today).

Bribery in Franklin County was a large-scale, highly organized industry. The kickback system began in 1928, when the county sheriff divided the territory into districts. Each district was supervised by a sheriff's deputy, who recruited new moonshiners and kept tabs on established operators. The fees were fixed at $25 per still and $10 for each batch of whiskey—

the equivalent of about $330 and $130 in modern money, and a sizable sum for moonshiners to pay. They had no choice, of course, since the system was administered by the commonwealth attorney, Carter Lee. The inflow of cash was so huge that county officials had to designate a full-time accountant and treasurer to keep track of it.

In 1934 the Treasury's Alcohol Tax Unit, responding to reports about the activities in Franklin County, dispatched an undercover agent to the area. The agent spent nearly a year collecting information on the bribery system, and a grand jury was ultimately convened. Thirty-four public officials were indicted in February 1935, including Carter Lee, despite the fact that Deputy Sheriff Thomas Jefferson Richards, a key prosecution witness, was assassinated several weeks before he could testify.

The Moonshine Conspiracy Trial lasted ten weeks and became a focus of national attention; the most prominent journalist to cover it was Sherwood Anderson. For the local population, it was the O.J. Simpson, Charles Manson, and Lindbergh baby kidnapping trials rolled into one. Although the government assembled a formidable case, they were hampered by the unseen connections of a tightly knit community, and allegations of jury tampering were widespread. Carter Lee happened to be the great-nephew of General Robert E. Lee, the most famous Virginian to date and a hero to the population, and no one believed he would be convicted. He wasn't. When the verdicts were announced on July 1, twenty of twenty-three defendants were found guilty and received light sentences; Lee and two others were acquitted. In the wake of the charges of jury tampering, a second trial was held in 1936, but this time most of the convicted men received a sentence of probation. Carter Lee was not indicted again.

Change came slowly to Franklin County, and it really wasn't until after World War II that enough industry penetrated the area to provide well-paying jobs that were an alternative to moonshining. Slightly more than 56,000 people live in the county today, and many commute to jobs in Lynchburg, Roanoke, or Danville. The area still calls itself the Moonshine Capital of the World, and some of that reputation may be justified. The largest still ever found in the county was busted in 1972. It was capable of producing nearly 1,500 gallons of whiskey per week; later that year, an even larger still was uncovered. No one was charged in either bust. Operation Lightning Strike, an anti-moonshine campaign conducted between 1999 and 2001, resulted in thirty indictments and the closing of several large-scale moonshine operations. Statistically, roughly half the illegal stills raided and destroyed in Virginia were located in Franklin County.

Aside from the income that moonshine brought to chronically poor farmers, the psychological impact of illegal moonshine was enormous and even incalculable. Simply put, moonshiners were heroes to local populations in the Appalachian hills—whether those populations were in the business themselves or not. Sympathies for still operators ran very deep. Remember that the Scots-Irish had been first driven out of Scotland by unfair taxation, then forced out of Northern Ireland for the same reason, and now it was the US government that wanted to put them out of business and toss them in jail. Other than informants equally desperate for cash, it was nearly impossible to find anyone who sided with the revenue men over their fellow citizens.

Remember, too, that many of those revenue men came from poor rural backgrounds themselves, and were not without sympathy for the offenders they were pursuing. If you subscribe to the often-repeated theory that police and criminals come from the same population pool, it's easy to envision how close some of the federal agents were to their targets; many of them probably had an uncle, cousin, or friend back home who augmented their income with the production of illicit whiskey. The government certainly subscribed to that theory: As time went on, more and more agents were drawn from the ranks of former moonshiners, with the assumption that they knew better than anyone else where the targets were. Over and over I heard stories about revenue men who tipped off moonshiners to the likelihood of impending raids, or who occasionally looked the other way to benefit a family in need.

First and foremost in Southern folklore, moonshiners were outlaws and outlaws were heroes. This was the fatal flaw in the government's pursuit of illegal still operators: Their ongoing efforts to stamp out illicit whiskey elevated moonshiners to near-mythical status. They were the people everyone else wanted to be—the rugged individualists who stood up against the system and told the government to shove it. As the nineteenth century blended into the twentieth and American society became more impersonal and industrialized, this image grew even more powerful. For the majority of the population in the Appalachian hills, it was probably their emotional equivalent of the *Rambo* movies. You might not be in a position to defy the system yourself, but you could certainly support and cheer on the efforts of those who did. If the moonshiners hadn't existed, some brilliant individual probably would have invented them. Ironically, they were anointed by their sworn enemies.

☆ ☆ ☆

DIXIE MAFIA

At 4:30 on the morning of August 12, 1967, Sheriff Buford Pusser was awakened by a phone call reporting a disturbance on the Tennessee-Mississippi border.

Pusser was the sheriff of McNairy County, Tennessee, which straddled the state line across from Alcorn County, Mississippi. Such calls were not unusual in rural law enforcement. There was no central switchboard or teams of patrol officers—if you were the guy in charge, you went out and handled trouble yourself. Pusser's wife, Pauline, frequently accompanied him on calls, and she insisted on going along this time. They got in the car and headed for the state line.

They drove directly into an ambush. When the Pussers reached the New Hope Church, a black car containing four men pulled out and followed them. The car came alongside the Pussers' vehicle and opened fire. Pauline was hit twice in the head and died immediately. Pusser's jaw was blown off; he was hospitalized and required a lengthy process of plastic surgery to reconstruct his face.

In the years and decades that followed, many members of the public became aware of an organization called the Dixie Mafia. They also became aware of Buford Pusser. The controversial and notorious sheriff was immortalized in a 1973 movie titled *Walking Tall*, which was loosely based on Pusser's life story. The film depicted Pusser as a crusader who didn't hesitate to apply his own brand of personal justice. This may or may not have been true in real life, depending on the sources you choose to believe. On one end of the spectrum, Pusser is viewed as a fearless lawman who continually risked his life in his quest to eliminate criminal activity in McNairy County—and in fact, he was knifed seven times and shot eight times during his tenure as sheriff. The opposite view holds that he was corrupt and violent, as evil as the men he was trying to eradicate. As usual the truth is probably somewhere in the middle, and largely hinges on which side of the law you view it from.

By anyone's standards, Buford Pusser had an interesting life. He was born in 1937 in McNairy County, where his father was police chief of Adamsville. He enlisted in the Marines after high school, but was given a medical discharge due to asthma. Pusser wrestled professionally before entering law enforcement—at six feet six inches and 250 pounds, his nickname was Buford the Bull. He eventually followed in his father's footsteps and became Adamsville's police chief, and served as sheriff of McNairy County from 1964 to 1970. He died in a car crash on August 21, 1974. History has been kind to him. The house he lived in at the time of his death is now the Buford Pusser Museum, and a Buford Pusser Festival is held each year in Adamsville. In 2004 a remake of *Walking Tall* starred professional wrestler Dwayne "The Rock" Johnson.

☆　☆　☆

The forerunner of the Dixie Mafia was the State Line Mob. They were a loosely knit group of thugs who migrated from Phenix City, Alabama, after the National Guard was called in to control the criminal element there. They clustered around the clubs along Highway 45, the line of demarcation between Tennessee and Mississippi. One of the first arrivals was Jack Hathcock, who began working at the State Line Club in 1936. The club was owned by local crime boss L. A. Timlake. Although just sixteen years old and recently released from the reformatory at Nashville, Hathcock quickly increased the club's take from illegal gambling and liquor. He met and married his wife, Louise, in 1937.

In the early 1940s Timlake was having trouble with the IRS, and sold the State Line Club to the Hathcocks. In the meantime McNairy County had gone dry, enabling the couple to make a handsome living selling bootleg booze. They had continual problems with the law throughout the 1940s—as did Jack's nephew, W. O. Hathcock Jr., who owned and operated the nearby Plantation Club.

There was a standard routine in the Hathcock joints. Tourists and traveling businessmen would seek out the clubs in search of a drink and some fun. They were enticed into the backroom casino, the site of rigged crap games, blackjack tables, and three-card monte. If they complained after being fleeced of all their money, they were beaten up and tossed out on the street; if they went to the police, they were killed. The bottom of the Tennessee River was reportedly filled with their cement-weighted bodies.

Despite a constant stream of bootlegging, violence, and murder, the Hathcocks appeared to be untouchable. Jack had paid off every politician he could find, from the governor on down. Every time he or one of his henchmen was indicted for something, the witnesses against them always seemed to withdraw or disappear. Even the occasional upright law enforcement officer posed no problem. When the heat on the State Line Club intensified in 1949, Jack dynamited the place and built a new club called the Forty-Five Grill. After Lyle Taylor became sheriff of Alcorn County in 1956, he immediately began a crusade against the Hathcocks, and succeeded in getting a court order to shut down the Forty-Five Grill. Jack engineered a scheme to sell the club to a local automobile dealer, after which he burned the club to the ground and bought the land back. Jack began construction of the Shamrock Restaurant and Motel on the property. The Shamrock opened in June 1957, and authorities estimated that the Hathcocks were netting $7,000 per week from their illegal activities.

In February 1957 Buford Pusser had just mustered out of the Marines, and headed to the Plantation Club for a good time. It's hard to imagine why he was there at all—three years earlier he had witnessed Louise Hathcock beating a sailor to death with a hammer at the Forty-Five, an incident he claimed haunted him for the rest of his life. This time around, Pusser almost ended up like the sailor. He got involved in a rigged crap game in the back room. After accusing the house of cheating, he was robbed and beaten by four of Hathcock's thugs and dumped on the street. It took 192 stitches to close his wounds. Pusser vowed to get revenge on the State Line Mob one day. It was the beginning of a long feud between him and the Hathcock family.

In the meantime, Louise had separated from Jack Hathcock. After their divorce, Jack begged her to stay on at the Shamrock and help him operate the business, which was booming. They settled into an uneasy relationship in which Jack alternated between neediness and jealousy. Louise began an affair with one of his employees, Pee Wee Walker. In June 1957 Walker's murdered body was found outside Corinth. Charges were filed against Hathcock, but nothing was ever proven, in spite of a widespread belief that he had paid for the hit.

Buford Pusser returned to the Plantation Club with two friends in December 1957. It was time to even the score with W. O. Hathcock. The three men waited until closing time, when the club was deserted, at which point they robbed the cash register and beat Hathcock, sending him to the hospital for weeks. They were later indicted for armed robbery and attempted murder, and acquitted.

Among the State Line Mob associates who hung out at the Hathcock joints, none was more unpredictable and dangerous than Carl Douglas "Towhead" White. White arrived at the state line in 1953 with one consuming ambition: to become the Southern equivalent of his idol, Al Capone. He dabbled in bootlegging and worked at the Forty-Five as a club enforcer, beating up customers who complained about losing money—something he truly enjoyed. After a stint in prison, he returned to the state line in 1957 and headed for the Shamrock. After the murder of Pee Wee Walker, White started his own affair with Louise Hathcock. He had no passion for her, but recognized that she was the person who controlled both the club and the money.

During the late 1950s and early 1960s, Towhead White drifted in and out of prison. He had graduated from bootlegging to armed robbery and contract killing. He married and divorced the same woman twice, which infuriated Louise, who was completely infatuated with him. Jack Hathcock wasn't pleased with his ex-wife's romance with White and constantly pressured her to drop him. Eventually the couple became fed up with Hathcock and hatched a plot to kill him.

On May 22, 1964, they retired to Louise's private quarters at the Shamrock and executed their plan. She allowed White to beat her up, then sent for her ex-husband. When Jack entered the room, White emerged from a corner and shot him to death. Louise telephoned the sheriff, informing him that Hathcock had assaulted her and that she had killed him in self-defense. She was charged with murder and released on bond. During the subsequent hearing, she said she had shot Hathcock in fear for her life; the sheriff testified that she had been badly beaten, and backed up her self-defense story. She was acquitted.

Towhead White became the leader of the State Line Mob. He held sway over Louise and had access to all of the Shamrock's profits, but there were problems looming for him. In September 1964 Buford Pusser was elected sheriff of McNairy County at the age of twenty-six. He had run on a promise to clean up the state line clubs once and for all. White knew that Pusser hated the Hathcocks, and he also knew the new sheriff would never accept a bribe. He began calling Pusser's office and house and threatening his family. In retaliation, Pusser handcuffed White, drove him down to the Hatchee River, and beat him up. He teamed up with the Alcorn County sheriff to raid the Shamrock, and kept harassing Louise Hathcock. Events escalated when White lured Pusser out to the woods to investigate a nonexistent moonshine still; while the sheriff searched for the still, White poured gasoline all over his patrol car and burned it to a crisp.

At this point White decided that it might not be wise to stick around the Shamrock and wait for Pusser's response. He started spending more and more time in Biloxi, Mississippi, where he linked up with the Dixie Mafia.

Like the State Line Mob, the Dixie Mafia was a loose association of career criminals. Branches of the organization thrived throughout the Appalachian South after World War II, starting out as groups of hoodlums who specialized in robbery, extortion, contract killing, moonshining, and bootlegging. For the most part they flourished in rural areas where law enforcement was sporadic. They differed from the Sicilian Mafia in a number of ways. Unlike the Sicilians, they had no common origin or nationality; their membership was drawn from any ethnic group with a penchant for criminal activity (African Americans aside, of course). They also had no formal hierarchy. The Dixie Mafia in various locales was usually led by the member who had the most money, provided that person was willing to kill anyone who got in his way. The one thing they shared with the Sicilians was the code of *omertà*, or silence. Their single unbreakable commandment was "Thou shalt not snitch to the cops," and anyone who violated it was eliminated at once.

The headquarters of the Dixie Mafia was Biloxi, Mississippi, specifically the area bordering the Gulf Coast known as The Strip—a boulevard of sleaze containing gambling dens, houses of prostitution, and nightclubs that offered both, washed down with bootleg liquor, very similar to Highway 45 on the state line. The Godfather of Biloxi was a Croatian immigrant named Mike Gillich, otherwise known as Mr. Mike. Gillich owned a string of clubs on The Strip, including the famous Golden Nugget. He was the glue that held the Dixie Mafia together, the one person that everyone in the organization trusted. He served as the post office, banker, and counselor for members in and out of Biloxi. He coordinated the payoffs to law enforcement that made his clubs nearly invincible. Most importantly, he was the protector of one of the Dixie Mafia's kingpins, Kirksey McCord Nix Jr.

Nix grew up in Oklahoma, the son of a prominent attorney who later became a state legislator and, ultimately, a judge. The elder Nix made his reputation by defending a succession of career criminals. He also vacationed in Biloxi, where he became friends with a young strip club owner named Mike Gillich. When his son joined the air force and was heading to Keesler Air Force Base in Biloxi, he told him to look up Mike Gillich if he ever got into trouble.

Kirksey Nix Jr. had a habit of getting into trouble from a young age, and introduced himself to Gillich immediately after arriving in town. He began spending his spare time in Mr. Mike's clubs on The Strip, and he was not alone. The twenty thousand airmen stationed at Keesler were a prime target for Biloxi's illegal gambling, and many of them lived in perpetual debt to people like Gillich. When Nix's one-year tour of duty was over, he stayed in Biloxi and worked with the Dixie Mafia. When he was not in Biloxi or out pulling a job, he stuck around Fort Smith, Arkansas. He was fond of frequenting a whorehouse run by a friend of his, Juanda Jones. Jones had an adolescent daughter, LaRa, who had a massive crush on Nix, and who would be involved with him on and off for several decades.

Towhead White became a lieutenant in the Dixie Mafia and made frequent trips to Biloxi to pull bank robberies with them. He organized a moonshine ring, bought a 1,500-gallon still, and was soon distributing illegal booze to contacts in Tennessee, Alabama, and Mississippi. He moved his still away from the state line to avoid harassment from Buford Pusser, but was busted in Mississippi and sent to prison for bootlegging.

On February 1, 1966, Sheriff Pusser arrived at the Shamrock Motel to arrest Louise Hathcock on a robbery complaint. Louise pulled a gun on him, and he shot her to death. The killing of Louise Hathcock was the culmination of the feud between Pusser,

White, and the Hatchcocks, and Towhead White swore he would get revenge. He emerged from prison late in 1966. Less than a month later Pusser was shot on Highway 45 near the Tennessee-Mississippi border, and White became the prime suspect. In reality, the sheriff had been shot by his girlfriend, a mulatto woman named Pearl, who was also carrying on with White. Towhead White surrendered and was returned to prison—the same prison that held Kirksey McCord Nix.

While there, he conspired with Nix to put a hit on Pusser. Nix recruited three other men to help him, and he and White planned the mechanics of the murder down to the last detail. When Nix got out, he went into action. On the evening of August 11, 1967, Kirksey Nix and his confederates checked into the Shamrock Motel. The phone rang in Sheriff Pusser's home at 4:30 the next morning, and he headed off to the state line with Pauline.

In the immediate aftermath of the assassination attempt that resulted in his wife's death, Buford Pusser identified Kirksey McCord Nix as the triggerman. He changed his story a few times in the following months—a strange thing for him to do, since law enforcement officials are always alert to discrepancies in stories when interrogating witnesses, and tend to regard those discrepancies as a warning sign of guilt. Two things were certain in his mind, however. He had sworn to himself to get even with his wife's killers if it took him the rest of his life, and he was also sure that Towhead White had been involved in commissioning and planning the attack.

White was released from prison once again in September 1968 with one overriding goal—to finish off Buford Pusser. He let the sheriff know he was back and that he would eventually be coming for him. Now that Louise was dead, he had no business connections in the state line area. His enthusiasm for the region was further diminished when Pusser visited his trailer outside of Corinth, pulled out a machine gun, and riddled the structure with bullets; White was miraculously unhurt, and the incident was never traced back to the sheriff. White shuttled back and forth between Alcorn County and Biloxi, where he spent his time doing bank robberies and contract murders with the Dixie Mafia.

According to W. R. Morris, who wrote a number of books on Buford Pusser and the State Line Mob, Pusser carefully planned the murder of Towhead White. He began by convincing Police Chief Art Murphy, an old friend, to arrange a private meeting between him and White so the two men could bury the hatchet. The meeting took place in March 1969. In the meantime Pusser was doing favors for Berry "Junior" Smith, a small-time hood who owned the El Rey Motel in Corinth along with his wife, Shirley. Pusser reportedly wanted Smith in his debt, and cut him numerous breaks on bootlegging violations. Early in April, Shirley Smith suggested to White that they get together and party, after which he could drop her back at the El Rey Motel. Shortly after midnight, White's Chrysler pulled into the El Rey parking lot. A sniper waited for him on the roof, armed with a .30-30 rifle. As Shirley flattened herself against the passenger door, a single bullet crashed through the windshield and hit White in the forehead.

Alcorn County Sheriff Grady Bingham got a report of gunshots at the El Rey and drove over to investigate. When he arrived, Junior Smith took responsibility for killing White. His story was that he and White had gotten into an argument, and White started shooting at him. Smith then supposedly ducked into the office, retrieved the .30-30 rifle and fired several times at White, after which he took a .357 magnum and shot numerous times at the car. Shirley Smith's story was identical to her husband's. Although it was obvious that the fatal shot had been fired from well above the ground, a grand jury accepted Smith's story of self-defense and refused to indict him.

Morris's theory was that Pusser had recruited Smith to take the fall for the crime, knowing that he would probably get off. Shirley Smith participated in the plot, and the hit man was hired by her husband. After the fatal shot, the killer handed the rifle down to Smith, who fired more bullets into the car. Many local people suspected that Pusser had been behind the murder. Law enforcement suspected it as well, but was delighted to be rid of Towhead White. Of the four men suspected to be in the car during Pusser's assassination attempt, three of them were killed in the years that followed—one in Boston, and two in Texas.

Kirksey McCord Nix kept rolling. He was arrested five times in 1968 on charges that included assault with intent to murder, bribing an officer, narcotics possession, auto theft, use of a stolen credit card, threatening witnesses, possession of burglary tools, and illegal possession of police radios. He got off every time. In February 1969 Nix and three confederates robbed a band of gypsies in Louisiana of $12,000 in cash and a considerable amount of jewelry. They executed one of the victims during the robbery, and the four were indicted for murder. To forestall trial, Nix surrendered himself on a minor charge in Atlanta; while he was in jail in Georgia, the body of the main witness against him in the murder case was found shot to death back in Louisiana. The charges were dropped, and Nix walked out of prison in 1970.

His luck ran out the following year. Nix was arrested for the murder of a New Orleans grocer named Frank Corso. He was tried, convicted, and sentenced to life in prison. After serving out the remainder of a previous sentence in Leavenworth, he was transferred to the Louisiana State Penitentiary at Angola. At that time Angola was one of the most notorious prisons in the United States, a place where inmates still worked on chain gangs under the watchful eyes of heavily armed guards. For Kirksey Nix, however, it was practically a resort. He paid off the prison hierarchy to get a soft job, which he paid other inmates to do on his behalf. He was then free to concentrate on his newest scam, a venture he entered into with fellow inmate Bobby Joe Fabian. It was a scheme that was to earn him millions of dollars, money that was earmarked for paying off high-ranking state officials to secure a pardon. It was also a venture that was to result in the deaths of more innocent people. As accomplished a criminal as he was on the outside, it was in Angola that Kirksey McCord Nix entered the annals of history.

☆   ☆   ☆

Well into the 1980s, Biloxi hadn't changed much. The Strip was still controlled by Mike Gillich, the authorities were still paid to look the other way, and the Dixie Mafia still treated the city as their home away from home.

Pete Halat was from the same immigrant neighborhood as Mike Gillich, but the two men had taken divergent paths. Halat went to law school, became a successful attorney, and eventually entered politics. His partner in his law practice was Vincent Sherry. Sherry had made a career out of defending the Dixie Mafia thugs who hung out in Gillich's clubs, but had an unblemished reputation himself. He left the law practice in 1986 to become a circuit court judge. His wife, Margaret, was known locally as a fearless crusader against corruption, and had frequently clashed with her husband over his defense of Biloxi criminals. She ran unsuccessfully for mayor in 1985 and was planning another campaign. She was also conducting an independent investigation that promised to blow the lid off Biloxi's municipal corruption.

On September 16, 1987, the bodies of Vince and Margaret Sherry were discovered in their house after the judge failed to appear for a full court docket. They appeared to have been the victims of a gangland-style execution. The Sherry's children rushed down to Biloxi. When their daughter Lynne arrived and met with Pete Halat, the attorney advised her not to look too closely into her parents' death—to accept it and leave it alone. Lynne Sherry Sposito was suspicious, and launched a probe that went on for over a decade.

Pete Halat was elected mayor of Biloxi in 1988, a post he likely would never have achieved if Margaret Sherry had remained alive. The closer Lynne Sposito and her private investigators got to the Sherry murders, the stranger they became. It turned out that one of Halat's clients was Kirksey McCord Nix. Although Halat had barely done any legal work for the criminal, he was acting as the administrator of Nix's bank accounts while Nix languished in Angola. Even stranger was the fact that a woman named LaRa Sharpe was working as an unpaid paralegal in Halat's office—the same woman who had met Kirksey Nix nearly two decades before in her mother's bordello outside Fort Smith, Arkansas. Lynne Sposito's investigators dug further and uncovered the scam Kirksey Nix had been running from prison.

In its own way, it was brilliant. Nix placed advertisements in gay newspapers and magazines, posing as a young gay man looking for companionship and love. The respondents who answered the ads tended to be older, wealthy, and desperate. Nix would first correspond with them, then call them on the prison phone for heart-to-heart conversations. In time, when the targets of the scam were comfortable and relaxed, he would ask for money for plane fare to come out and visit. If the mark sent the plane fare, a string of misfortunes would follow: The young gay man had been arrested en route and needed bail money to get out of jail. If that worked, Nix kept milking the mark until he wised up and stopped sending money. The scam was perfect in a number of ways. It was the early 1980s, a period in America when homosexuality was not generally condoned or accepted, and the target was not likely to complain. If he was still in the closet, which was likely at that time, Nix could come back and blackmail him later.

His success was remarkable. At its height the gay lonely-hearts scam grossed at least half a million dollars annually, and some estimates put Nix's take into the millions. Nix had dozens of associates scattered around the country, picking up Western Union money orders from mail drops in exchange for 10 or 15 percent of the proceeds, plus expenses. All the money was being channeled through the Halat and Sherry law firm—unknown to Vincent Sherry—and processed by LaRa Sharpe and Pete Halat. The proceeds were earmarked to buy Nix's pardon from corrupt Louisiana officials.

In early 1987 Kirksey Nix made an alarming discovery. A large sum of money was missing from his scam bank accounts, close to half a million dollars. He went ballistic and promised to kill whoever was involved in skimming the money. Pete Halat drove to Angola to meet with the enraged Nix, and blamed the theft on Vince Sherry. He helped Nix concoct the murder plot on one condition: Margaret Sherry had to die as well. Back in Biloxi, Mike Gillich served as the point man to hire the killer and arrange the hit.

It took Lynne Sposito ten years, a pile of money, and an endless supply of heartache to bring her parents' killers to justice, but she finally did. Pete Halat was tried and convicted for his role in the murders. Mike Gillich was indicted as well, and to everyone's astonishment turned state's evidence and testified. Mr. Mike's abandonment of the code of *omertà* was an unmistakable signal that times had changed, and his reign of terror was over. He served nine years of a twenty-year sentence, was released from prison in 2000, and died in 2012 at the age of eighty-two. A nurse and mother of three had finally succeeded in bringing down the Dixie Mafia.

As of this writing, Kirksey McCord Nix is still sitting in Angola. He has never admitted complicity or involvement in the Sherry killings. After the details of the lonely-hearts scam were uncovered, he was moved to an isolation cell where he is barred from contact with the outside world.

Part 2:

THE MODERN MOONSHINERS

☆ ☆ ☆

PIEDMONT DISTILLERS AND THE LEGACY OF JUNIOR JOHNSON

The hills of North Carolina played host to moonshiners from the earliest days of colonial America, going back to the time when the first Scots-Irish settlers migrated down the Appalachian Trail from the Northeast.

It's no surprise, then, that the state was one of the first to legalize the production and sale of moonshine—provided the still operator paid his taxes, of course. Joe Michalek, a transplanted New Yorker, founded Piedmont Distillers in 2005. Michalek was a marketing and advertising man who had moved down a decade earlier to work with R. J. Reynolds. His moment of awakening came one night during a blues jam session out in the woods, when someone passed around a jar of peach moonshine.

He remembers having a host of questions as the jar circulated toward him: Should I drink it? Is it safe? Will it make me go blind? At the first sip, his qualms disappeared with the realization that this was one of the smoothest things he had ever tasted, and one of the best. He was hooked—not just on the taste of the whiskey, but also on the history and romance of it. His first product, Catdaddy Carolina Moonshine, was a spiced, corn-based moonshine that became an instant hit and still has a cult following today.

North Carolina may or may not have been the place where moonshine originated, but it definitely was the birthplace of NASCAR. Through his work at Reynolds, Michalek had met Junior Johnson, the legendary bootlegger and race car driver. Johnson had not only been the king of the track, but also came from one of the biggest moonshining families in the state. Michalek

Junior Johnson, legendary moonshiner and NASCAR driver, next to his bootleg car—a rebuilt 1940 Ford. COURTESY JUNIOR JOHNSON PERSONAL COLLECTION

began to pursue Junior to go into partnership with him, convinced that the Johnson family recipe—not to mention the hard-charging Johnson mystique—would be an unbeatable market combination. Junior Johnson's Midnight Moon was launched in 2007, and today Piedmont Distillers produces nearly two of every three bottles of moonshine consumed in America.

Here's how it all started, according to Junior: Sunday was the bootleggers' day off, the one day of the week when they didn't haul shine up and down the back roads of Wilkes County. They would get together and race.

"It was really just about seein' who had the fastest car," he explains. "A lot of 'em was bootleggers like I was and they had fast cars, but the only ones that came close to mine was when Red Vogt was there from Atlanta. They were all just seein' if they could outrun the other guy."

Vogt was one of the greatest stock car mechanics who ever lived, the man behind Red Byron and the Raymond Parks racing team that would later dominate the early days of NASCAR. For his part, Junior had been driving around the Johnson farm since the age of nine, and running moonshine since he was fourteen. One Sunday, as he was plowing a field with the family's farm mule, his brother came up to him and asked if he wanted to race; he said sure, why not, but had to go back to the house and get his shoes first.

The weekly races began to draw larger and larger local crowds. It was casual, unregulated, and fun. Everything changed, however, after Bill France got involved. France was a driver turned race promoter, and very early on saw the commercial possibilities of racing. Although there were a number of competing racing series and promoters at the time, he was determined to make his circuit the dominant force in stock car racing.

"When Bill found out that the Wilkes County guys was bootleggers, he realized they had the money and the fast cars. Nobody else had any money, really, and France had to get to it to get his racing goin'. He hung around North Wilkesboro for six months or a year, maybe longer—married a local girl while he was up there. But he kept hangin' around until he found the ten or twelve boys that made all the money in the whiskey business, and that's what got him started. They used the money they made from liquor to build the racetracks."

In 1947 France convened a meeting of drivers at the Streamline Hotel in Daytona and founded the National Association for Stock Car Auto Racing, or NASCAR. Junior didn't participate much at first— the purses were small, and he was making too much money hauling shine. But when he finally got involved, he was unbeatable.

"Remember that I was doin' the racin' with my moonshine cars. I had to have those things strong enough to haul twenty-two six-gallon cases that weighed 1,200 or 1,400 pounds, and you had to outrun the law carryin' that. You had to put on big tires, big wheels, two shocks on every wheel, and you had to be fast enough to get away from 'em every time."

I ask him how fast they were going in the early days.

"Couldn't tell," he grins, "'cause the speedometer only went up to 100. But I'd guess 125, somethin' like that."

Later in the day, in Charlotte, I walk through the NASCAR Hall of Fame with Junior and Michalek; he was inducted into the Inaugural Class in 2010. The experience is similar to taking a stroll across the Red Sea with Moses. Roughly every ten feet, we're stopped by a tourist—a fan who wants to shake his hand, get his autograph, or pose with him in a picture. He is unfailingly polite, and obviously enjoys it. The Hall is organized in a winding circular pattern, with vintage race cars arrayed in chronological order around a simulated track. The exhibits begin with Red Byron's 1940 Ford. We stop in front of Lee Petty's car.

"He was a good driver," says Junior, "but he was a dirty driver. If he was behind you with five or six laps to go in the race, he's spin you out. He wouldn't hesitate to do it to you. He did it to me twice. Then the last time I was drivin' at the Charlotte Fairgrounds, I was sittin' on the

Agents posing with some of the haul of the largest moonshine bust in North Carolina history: more than 7,000 gallons captured at the home of Glenn Johnson, Junior's father, in the 1930s. COURTESY JUNIOR JOHNSON PERSONAL COLLECTION

pole and Lee was outside of me. I purposely let him beat me out at the start. Then I took him down on the third turn of the very first lap—sent him out through the fence," he laughs, "and he hit a big oak tree head on. From then on he begged me not to wreck him again. But he was a mean rascal when it came down to a few laps to go. He'd just wreck you."

"What about Richard Petty?" asks Michalek. "What was his style?"

"He was different. If he couldn't beat you, he wouldn't wreck you."

"I heard Lee was in the bootlegging business," says Michalek.

"He was. Pretty heavy at one time. He'd support his race car with it."

A number of exhibits are devoted to Junior. There is a section re-creating the glory days at North Wilkesboro Speedway, his home track, and a number of cars that he financed in his days as the owner of his own racing team. Junior was more than just a money man, however—one classic photograph shows him swinging a ninety-pound jack from one side of the car to the other, in an effort to save precious seconds. We pass Cale Yarborough's Cutlass, the car that won three consecutive championships (1976–78) for the Johnson team. On the third floor there is a replica of an old-time moonshine still, constructed by Junior for the Hall. We sit down in front of the still and he describes the operation in detail. In the background, a movie narrates the history of NASCAR and Bill France; in the early days, France's appearance resembled a country version of Errol Flynn. I ask Junior if he thinks the past is being sugar-coated just a bit.

"Yep," he chuckles. "They made a movie 'bout me, too."

He's referring to The Last American Hero, *a film that came out in 1973. The title was taken from Tom Wolfe's breakout piece in* Esquire *in 1965. Junior was played by Jeff Bridges.*

"Was it accurate, do you think?"

"It was a movie," he smiles. "'Bout as accurate as you could do in Hollywood, I guess."

☆   ☆   ☆

When Piedmont Distillers launched Junior Johnson's Midnight Moon in 2007, moonshine was very far from a national trend. In fact, it was not on anyone's radar screen in the spirits industry. Unlike wine, spirits marketing is top-down: A bunch of very rich and influential individuals get together, decide what next year's hot category will be, and spend enough money to make it happen. In this context, Joe Michalek was either a visionary or a crazy person.

"After that first taste of moonshine out in the woods," he says, "I was blown away by the quality of it, and wondered why no one was selling it legally. I also believed that anything that had this much history, love, and mystique behind it had the potential to become a very powerful idea."

He turned out to be a visionary, as moonshine gradually morphed into one of the few consumer-led trends in the spirits business. We can speculate endlessly about the reasons why this happened: Perhaps people were bored, or fed up with products that had no personality; perhaps they were yearning for a lost America; perhaps they just needed more excitement in their lives. The one person who wasn't surprised, interestingly enough, was Junior.

"I was always the kind of person who never made a mistake," he told me. "I couldn't afford to. So I thought out everything I was gonna do. Very few of my projects failed."

This one certainly didn't, against the conventional wisdom of the spirits gurus. The upward trajectory of Piedmont Distillers has been astonishing: From 25,000 six-pack cases in 2010, the brand went to 75,000 in 2011 and 270,000 in 2012. By 2013 they were on track to sell their one-millionth case. It's a success story virtually unparalleled in the liquor business—at least without the support of a multinational beverage conglomerate and the millions of dollars of marketing help they can provide.

It has also been a remarkable journey in another respect. Given the drive, energy, and necessary financing, anyone can grow larger; the challenge is whether you can get bigger and not compromise your quality standards. Piedmont has managed to sustain unparalleled growth without sacrificing the integrity of their product, which is important in more than one respect. Given their dominant market position, Midnight Moon is likely to be the first bottle of moonshine a consumer tries—and unless they like it, they won't buy moonshine again.

The following day we head for the distillery. Junior is in his eighties now and his health has been fragile in recent years, so he has a driver—a guy named Kenny who used to work on his racing team. We pile into a huge Mercedes; Kenny is at the wheel, Michalek is next to him, and I sit in the back with Junior to pick his brain about the early days of NASCAR. I remind him that the last time we spoke, several years earlier, he indicated that his relationship with Bill France had been a difficult one.

"Well, it was a relationship where they felt they needed to control me. They wanted to stop me from gettin' too much of an advantage, so they'd do everything they could to slow me down. But they didn't do a very good job," he smiles, "'cause I just kept on outsmartin' 'em.

"But most of the stuff I was doin' had to do with safety, not speed. I was interested in savin' my own neck. In the beginning, of course, you could put any kind of car out there you wanted to. But as time went on, the inspectors got stricter and stricter. They needed to have a rule for everything. I went to Daytona one year with a car that had the two back wheels tilted 3 degrees, so when they went through the turn, they'd be sittin' flat on the racetrack. It had more traction than anyone else had, but they didn't know what it was for. So they took it away from me, and now all the cars are usin' it. So I had a much harder time than anyone else did, 'cause I had to outsmart NASCAR as well as all the other drivers.

"The problem was that if you had a safety innovation, you had to prove to France that it worked. And of course, you couldn't prove it without runnin' it first. Many times NASCAR said I was cheatin', but I wasn't cheatin'—I was just tryin' to extend my life. I was on the track the day Fireball Roberts got killed, and it was the most awful thing I've ever seen. Once you see somethin' like that, you never want to see it again. My cars were safer than anybody else's—I had steel roller bars in 'em, braces, that kind of stuff. If I'd been buildin' my cars the same way other people were, I think I'd have been killed pretty early on. So I was just constantly innovatin', lookin' for anything that would give me an edge."

"This is a huge point," says Michalek, turning around to face us. "That was the life blood of the flippin' sport. People were always advancing and progressing, and at the end of the day it was in the DNA of you guys to try to innovate and stay ahead of the law. And

Moonshine Nation

everybody liked to see the drama of what was happening, of who was outsmarting the other guy. That's what the bootleggers brought to the sport. And that's why ratings are down now and people are less interested—they can no longer see that drama unfolding."

"That's right," says Junior.

"So of course you weren't cheating," adds Michalek. "You were innovating, and they thought you were cheating because they couldn't understand it. It was an interesting deal."

"Yeah," laughs Junior. "But when you come up with a better puzzle than anybody else and they don't have a rule for it, they don't like it much. Bill France Jr., in his last days, apologized to me for tryin' to control me. He told me it was the only way they could keep racin' even."

"Tell me about the old days in Daytona, back in the 1940s," I ask him. "That must have been wild."

"It was," he says. "Probably the wildest part was out on the beach. A lot of people didn't know how to run on that sand—a lot of 'em was new to racin' anyway, and it was totally different than asphalt. It took some skill."

"The sand must have been incredibly hard."

"Well, they always ran the race when the tide was out. The further you got out toward the water, the faster you could go. That's how I was outrunnin' 'em. You had to find the ruts the other drivers had made, to get your traction."

"Where were the spectators?"

"They were all along the beach. They'd park their cars, and there was a line where they couldn't get too close to the race. But there weren't any stands, 'cept at the North Turn."

"Whose idea was it to run part of the race out on the sand?"

"It was a couple of guys who hooked up with Bill France, Sr. In those days he didn't have the money to guarantee the purses for the drivers. So he'd team up with a local car dealership, and they'd put their name on the cars. Some of the guys didn't even have the money to get to the next race, and France would have to advance it to them.

"It was a hard thing for France," he says. "He was a Hollywood movie star type of person—he had the looks, but he didn't have any money. He was honest with the people he worked with; he had to be. But he knew how to have most of the good stuff slide to him, and of course you can't blame him."

I ask him if he thinks there's too much money in NASCAR today.

"The prices for the cars and parts is just humongous. I would say one of them cars probably costs millions now."

"Do you think that's why the appeal of the sport is eroding?"

"It costs too much to go to a race now, and some of 'em is just too long. They've backed down on their prices a lot, but they were up to $400 or $500, dependin' on where you sit. You know, most race fans have a regular job, and they can't afford to take their wife and kids to somethin' like that. It's just too expensive. I think it hit its peak, and they'll have to do somethin' to revive its standing."

Is that why he thinks the sport has changed—too much money?

"That, and somethin' else I don't think anybody knows. How can I explain it? You've got a different kind of driver now. All of them been to school." He pauses. "It's just not a he-man sport right now."

☆   ☆   ☆

We pull up in front of Piedmont's new distillery, and the contrast with the recent past is startling. The gleaming new building looks like a car dealership—which in fact it was, in a previous incarnation. The first time I came here, in 2011, they were making moonshine out of the old train depot in Madison. The still was shoehorned into one small room, with barely enough space to walk around. There was one bottling line back then; now there are eight.

Michalek gives me a tour of the facility. It started as a single building and morphed into a compound, with five more structures added during the expansion period. Two giant, ten-thousand-gallon custom-made stills are flanked by a group of large mashing tanks. There are buildings for blending, dry storage, fruit storage, and finished goods, but these are really just staging areas; there are three off-site warehouses as well. Piedmont bottles a number of Midnight Moon fruit infusions—Cherry, Strawberry, Blueberry, Cranberry, Blackberry, and Apple Pie—and the company is currently using over eleven thousand pounds of fruit per week.

"We moved here from the train depot somewhere around February of 2012, thinking that we'd be set for three to five years." He laughs. "The growth was so explosive that it was hard to keep product in the pipeline. We weathered the storm and got to where we are today, but it took tremendous effort on the part of the entire company. We had people working seven days a week, then working a second shift on top of that. We ran seven days a week from October 2012 to Memorial Day 2013; we had bottling lines ordered and coming in every two weeks, and we were hiring bottling teams and training them so that we could put that line into service the day it came in.

"It was a very dynamic time," he says. "Honestly, it was exhausting. But because we focus on quality of ingredients as well as tradition, it was impossible for us just to push a button and change our output. What makes us different is also what makes it tough for us to simply turn the volume knob."

We walk into the bottling room, and the full impact of the expansion hits me. The space is roughly the size of a hangar for a fleet of small aircraft. All eight lines are in production, manned by teams of eight to ten people. The din is tremendous. Michalek moves slowly through the room and greets every employee by name. He thanks them, slaps them on the back, tells them about the likelihood of hitting one million cases sometime during the fourth quarter, and stresses to each one that the credit belongs solely to them. It's an impressive exercise in motivational management, and it seems to be working. Without exception the employees are cheerful, upbeat, involved in their work, and proud of their product.

"We're using 100-percent restaurant-quality gourmet fruit," he shouts over the noise of the bottling lines. "Our products are significantly more expensive to make—because of the materials and the proof level, but also because we want to deliver a true moonshine experience. When you drink our product, it tastes like the fruit—as it should. That taste was the reason I got involved with this in the first place."

I ask him how he convinced Junior to become a partner.

"I had worked with him when I was at Reynolds, so we had some contact then. After we launched Catdaddy we approached him with the idea, but he was uncertain about it. Then about nine months later, I get a call from the distillery saying that Junior Johnson had a friend that wanted to see what it would take to go legit, and he wanted to come up the next day and see the operation. He walked through the place, met the people and saw what we were doing; I asked again if he'd be interested in working together, and he said he would take a look at it. So I developed some prototypes and came up with the Midnight Moon name, and he tasted it with all of his bootlegging buddies, and we were on our way.

"When he got involved, it really elevated our presence and helped us get the product on the shelf. Things became much easier because of his family history and his access to the motor sports world; it also made it easier for states to approve us for distribution. Basically, we took Junior out of retirement and put him back to work, and the thing snowballed. Things like that *Moonshiners* show on TV grew out of that, and all of it increased public awareness and helped get the concept on people's minds.

"One thing I can tell you," he says as we emerge from the bottling room out into the sunlight. "When we do hit a million cases, we'll throw one hell of a company party, with music and barbecue—and moonshine, of course."

☆   ☆   ☆

As the Mercedes rolls past the gently sloping hills toward Wilkes County, I ask Junior about his father's moonshine operation.

"I always thought my dad was the smartest person I'd ever seen, and I still believe that. He never varied from being a perfectionist. And I think a little bit of that grew on me."

Johnson Senior had the reputation for making the best moonshine in the county, and he grew all his own corn—the original grain-to-glass distiller. I ask how much whiskey he was turning out in his day.

"He had a deal where he'd furnish two other people with the equipment and all the materials to make it, and they'd go thirds on the profits. Altogether, he made 'bout three or four thousand gallons a week." *This was a huge amount, enough to put his father in the first rank of moonshiners.* "But it was hard times during the Depression. There used to be an old guy who went around sellin' seeds for things like potatoes and turnips. One time he came to my dad's place early on, and he had two friends there with him. The three of them ordered 'bout thirty-five cents worth. When the man came back the next week with the seeds, the three of them couldn't raise thirty-five cents. So you see why people went into bootleggin' to survive."

"Did he finally get out of the business?"

"Naw, he died in the liquor business. He was arrested and went to jail five times. He got three two-year sentences, one three-year sentence, and a five-year sentence." *The five-year sentence was for the largest moonshine bust in county history, when 7,100 gallons were captured at Johnson's home in 1936.* "You'd serve 'bout a third of that time. They'd usually parole a bootlegger out, since they figured he really wasn't a danger to anybody."

I tell him about the research I've been doing and ask if he knew Percy Flowers in Johnston County, the supposed King of the Moonshiners.

"Yeah," *he smiles.* "I dealt with Percy. He was the most hot-tempered man I ever seen. Lord Almighty, he had a temper. He liked them foxhounds, was a big dog man—had coon dogs and coyote dogs."

"When you dealt with him, were you buying or selling?"

"Buyin'. I had a customer down there and it was too far for me to haul, so I hired a boy to buy it from Percy and take it to my customer. His daughter still runs his operation, don't she?"

"Actually, she's turned the land into a gated community with a golf course."

Both Junior and Michalek find this to be hysterical.

"She calls me every once in a while," says Junior. "She has some functions she wants me to go to, and I went to two or three of 'em."

"Fund-raisers," laughs Michalek.

I tell them about Percy Flowers's sanitized Internet profile, and how his bio on the Flowers Plantation website never mentions moonshine.

"She wouldn't give me an interview, though. I get the impression that she wants to erase that whole period and pretend that it never existed."

"Well," Junior grins, "I don't believe she's gonna live that long."

"You knew Popcorn Sutton too, didn't you?" asks Michalek. "What was his deal?"

"They make him out to be a big moonshiner, but he wasn't very big—just a one-man operation doin' everything himself. I knew him for a long time. He come to some of the races in the early days."

"Why don't you tell him what you heard after Popcorn died?" asks Michalek.

"Well, they said he'd died and was gonna be buried the next day. I knew one of the guys that was supposed to have hauled him to the burial ground. I was out at Bristol gettin' ready for the race, and this guy comes up to me and says, 'Old Sutton's in the ground. I buried him this mornin' 'bout six o'clock.' I said, 'You buried him by yourself?' And he said yeah, the guy at the funeral home told him there was no sense waitin', just go ahead and put him in the ground." He laughs. "So I'll bet the son of a bitch is still alive."

"They've done a great job of marketing him," I observe. "They've really turned him into a hillbilly legend."

"That's the truth," chuckles Junior. "That's the goddang truth. But I think it's a little bit because he was a crazy feller, and people like that."

The car finally approaches Ingle Hollow, the place where it all started, and edges toward the old Johnson family farm. It's the first time Junior has been up here in ten years. He sold the house some years ago to his brother, and his nephew lives there now.

"You see that tree down yonder where the mountain looks trimmed?" He points toward the far hills. "Plumb on back that way, my dad owned every bit of that land. All the mountains, 'bout eight hundred acres." He looks up at the ridge and smiles. "See that blue haze up there in them hills? I 'spect they might be makin' some liquor up there."

"How much illegal distilling still goes on?" I ask him.

"There's a lot of people that make it for themselves, and then they let it leak out if they think they have a real good product. But there's very few people that put the effort into it, to make it safe and make it the same way every time."

The Mercedes snakes slowly around the hills toward the farm. Some of the road is paved, but often it's gravel or even dirt.

"Here we go," he says as we come up an incline. "That's my old house there. All this around here was my farm. And these were the roads I practiced race drivin' on, from here all the way back to the house. My dad used to let me take the car out from the time I was 'bout nine. The roads was crooked and they was all dirt. That's how I used to time *myself. It was 'bout a mile from here back to the house, and I'd look at the clock when I started, go down to the end of the road, spin around and come back. It was good practice for outrunnin' the law.*

"All these folks 'round here are kin to me," he says as we head back down the hill. "That's my grandpa's house over there."

"What did he do?"

"He was in the whiskey business too."

We pass a deep ravine overlooking a stream, about four hundred yards from the house.

"That was where they caught me," he says. "It was 1955, and I had just turned pro. I won a race in Altamonte, New York, and drove all night to get home. I come in 'bout four or four-thirty in the mornin', and my dad had overslept. He asked me to go out and fire up the still. You needed to do it before daylight, so nobody could see the smoke. So I went up to the still, and I was shovelin' a load of coke—you always wanted to use coke, 'cause it made less smoke. I was leanin' on the trough with the shovel, and when I stood up I caught a glimpse of somebody standin' on a box, gettin' ready to jump on my shoulders. It was a revenue man by the name of John West, and he was gonna jump right on top of my back. So I hit him on the head as hard as I could with that shovel, and away I went. He came out of the still hollerin', 'It's Junior Johnson—he just hit me with a shovel!' There was eighteen officers surrounding the place. My dad, my brother, and my uncle was comin' toward the still, and when they heard all the racket they had to head back toward the house. But the still was on my dad's land and close to the house, so they got him too."

Junior was sentenced to two years and served eleven months in the federal prison in Chillicothe, Ohio. It was a supreme irony for someone who had spent years outrunning the law, who at his height had seventy-five people on his payroll and ran tractor-trailers full of moonshine back and forth to New Orleans and Gulfport, Mississippi. He was granted a presidential pardon by Ronald Reagan in 1986.

"This was the heart of the liquor business in Wilkes County right here," he says as we turn onto Route 421, the old Bootlegger's Highway. The winding road is paved now, but back in Junior's time it was all dirt. "There wasn't a house along here that wasn't involved with the liquor business, one way or another. I used to take these curves at one-twenty, one-thirty," he says. "We'd go back and forth just 'bout every night."

I observe that it shouldn't have been too hard for the revenuers to catch them, if they always traveled on the same road at the same time.

"Yep, they could just sit and watch for you. But they'd never block the road so you couldn't get through—you could always get around them."

"Why do you think they never blocked the road?"

"They were afraid you wouldn't stop," he grins. "But their cars could never run fast enough to catch us. They used to get themselves a fast car every now and then, when they captured one in a raid, but they couldn't drive 'em. They'd just chase you, hopin' you'd blow up or wreck. And anyway, we were takin' all sorts of chances, 'cause if were caught we were goin' to jail. The revenue men didn't take any chances. It was just a job for them."

We leave Ingle Hollow and continue on 421 toward the old North Wilkesboro Speedway, the track many people consider to be the birthplace of NASCAR. It opened in 1947, with a promise from Bill France to hold races there in exchange for a cut of the gate. The track flourished for decades, but in the 1970s and 1980s NASCAR began to favor larger, more modern venues capable of generating bigger

Moonshine Nation

profits. In 1997 Bruton Smith moved the race from North Wilkesboro to his new track in Texas, and it closed down. The Speedway reopened briefly in 2010, but by the time I saw it in the summer of 2011 it was abandoned once again.

As we drive in, we can see the faded Winston Cup lettering on the old wooden grandstand. The gate is padlocked at the entrance.

"Looks like we're not getting in," says Michalek.

"Why don't you try that lock?" asks Junior. "I'll bet we can get in."

Michalek gets out and dutifully tries the lock, but the gate is impenetrable.

"Kenny, let's go down the road a bit," says Junior. "We can get in the back way."

We circle around the country roads and come in the back entrance, but that gate is locked as well. We're sitting in the middle of the infield, or what used to be the infield on race day. When Tom Wolfe came down here in 1965 to do his breakout piece on Junior for Esquire *("The Last American Hero is Junior Johnson. Yes!"), the place was a vortex of activity, with traffic extending for ten miles in every direction from North Wilkesboro Speedway on Sunday morning. Now we're surrounded by overgrown weeds and complete silence.*

"Was this the first NASCAR track?" asks Michalek.

"Either this or Martinsville," says Junior. "They were a month apart."

"What was the seating capacity?"

"'Bout four thousand to start. Forty-five thousand at the peak, but they never had it filled but once. It was my last race before I retired. I won the race. It was Richard Petty's second race."

It's obvious that Junior doesn't want to leave. He keeps staring at the abandoned grandstand.

"If somebody could open it up and run trucks or something," he says wistfully, "I bet they could build it back up."

At the new Piedmont Distillers facility in Madison, I sit down in a conference room with Joe Michalek to taste some moonshine. We begin with Catdaddy, the product that enabled Piedmont to make its bones. The attractive nose exudes cinnamon and nutmeg notes; there's a profusion of baking spices in the mouth, with a peppery edge in the mid-palate that turns sweet on the finish. It's Christmas in a glass, and extremely appealing.

With the Midnight Moon products, the fruit infusions are the clear winners—but at this point, of course, I've already seen the gourmet-quality fruit going into the jars on the bottling line. The Apple Pie, their largest seller, has sweet cinnamon aromas on the nose, followed by a tart mid-palate filled with mouthwatering acidity and a long, spicy finish. The Cherry is remarkable: tart and sweet, lush and opulent, richly textured, spicy and splendid. The Midnight Moon Original offers soft corn notes and firm alcohol scents on the nose. It's more flavorful in the mouth than the nose would lead you to expect, and has a nice peppery edge.

"I know the category is popular right now," says Michalek, "and a lot of people are jumping in. But many of them are making a different kind of product—they're not high-proof, and they're using extracts and coloring rather than real fruit. If your proof is lower, say 40 or 60 rather than 100 like ours, you'll obviously save money on excise taxes. But you end up with something totally different. It's almost like a ready-to-drink cocktail. So I think our

Moonshine Nation

product will stand up to them and survive, because of all the extra expense and effort we go through.

"Our whole reason for being is quality. What you're tasting now is basically what I tasted that night in the woods. It's what intrigued me so much about moonshine—except, of course, that our stuff is triple-distilled, and it's a grain neutral spirit."

I asked him why he decided to use grain neutral spirits (GNS) as opposed to a corn whiskey.

"We did a lot of taste tests, and the people who participated always told us that they preferred the purity of the neutral spirit. We tried a 160-proof corn, and we did all the flavors with it, but people said unanimously that they wanted neutral. We used all sorts of different recipes and fiddled with the sweetness level, but always came back to the theory that we wanted the fruit to shine through."

"Who's your customer? Are you targeting whiskey drinkers, or focusing on the recreational drinker who's migrating into spirits from another category?"

"Moonshine has been made in North Carolina and around the country for decades," he says. "For centuries, actually. Our customers are buying into the American heritage. It's the history and the intrigue. And while a lot of people may buy it initially because of the intrigue factor, we're getting our repeat business because of the juice in the jars.

"Our demographics tell us that the whole category of moonshine isn't a regional thing. It's an American thing. What comes back to us is that the people who engage in our brand are all over the board—51 percent male, 49 percent female, representing virtually every group and ethnic category out there. It's people from the South, of course, but also Oregon and Washington, New Hampshire, Texas, and California. It goes from bikers to bankers. Our customers look like America."

RECIPES
Courtesy of Piedmont Distillers

Moonshine Mule

1½ ounces Midnight Moon Original
1 ounce ginger beer
¾ ounce fresh lemon juice
1 ounce simple syrup

Pour all ingredients in a rocks glass over ice and stir gently.

Old-Fashioned Apple Pie

Orange slice
1½ ounces Midnight Moon Apple Pie
1½ ounces rye whiskey
5 dashes Boker's bitters

Muddle orange slice at the bottom of an old-fashioned glass. Fill glass with ice and add all other ingredients. Stir gently.

Blueberry Basilito

4 basil leaves
2 teaspoons sugar
2 tablespoons sparkling water
1½ ounces frozen blueberries
1½ ounces Midnight Moon Blueberry
2 tablespoons lime juice

Place basil, sugar, and sparkling water in a highball glass and muddle lightly. Add blueberries, crush and stir. Add ice, Midnight Moon Blueberry, and lime juice. Stir gently and serve with a straw.

Chocolate Cherry Moon

1½ ounces Midnight Moon Cherry
¾ ounce dark crème de cacao
3–4 dashes Bitter Truth chocolate molé bitters
½ ounce half and half

Shake all ingredients vigorously with ice for 15–20 seconds. Strain into rocks glass and garnish with dark chocolate shavings.

Frozen Cranberry Moonshine Lemonade

¾ cup Midnight Moon Cranberry
1 (12-ounce) can frozen lemonade concentrate
⅓ cup whole berry cranberry sauce
1 ounce orange liqueur
1 ounce lime juice

In a blender, combine all ingredients and fill with ice to 5-cup level. Process until smooth. Makes 5 cups.

Southern 75

1½ ounces Catdaddy
½ ounce lemon juice
½ ounce simple syrup
1 ounce brut Champagne
Twist of lemon

Mix Catdaddy, lemon juice, and simple syrup in a shaker. Shake over ice and pour into rocks glass over ice. Top with Champagne and garnish with a lemon twist. To serve straight up, strain into a martini glass.

Kitty Carlisle

¾ ounce Catdaddy
¾ ounce bourbon
¾ ounce fresh lemon juice
¾ ounce white crème de cacao

Shake all ingredients with ice for 30 seconds and strain into a small cocktail glass.

☆ ☆ ☆

SPENCER BALENTINE'S SILVER TRAIL DISTILLERY

To understand Spencer Balentine, you first have to grasp the significance of the Land Between the Lakes.

The two lakes are Kentucky Lake and Lake Barkley, man-made bodies of water created when the Cumberland and Tennessee Rivers were dammed up by the TVA, or Tennessee Valley Authority, in the 1950s and '60s. The LBL today is a national recreation area, supervised by the USDA Forest Service. No one lives there, but the area is a popular vacation destination for families and outdoor enthusiasts, who take advantage of the opportunities for fishing, hunting, camping, and racing OHVs (off-highway vehicles).

The former residents of the LBL, however, see those 170,000 acres very differently. The area was once their home, a close-knit community with its own heritage and traditions. Several small towns were located there, including Golden Pond (no relation to the movie of the same name). After the federal government decided to convert it to a national recreation area, they seized the land by right of eminent domain. The residents were paid pennies on the dollar for their homes and land and were unceremoniously kicked out.

"Our farm had been in the family 'bout one hundred years," recalls Spencer, who was a child at the time. "The back story to all this is that Alvin Barkley, the vice president, was from Paducah. He set the land aside during World War II for an alternate White House, and got the money put aside for it. As time went by and FDR died, the money was still there, but he couldn't get anybody to do anything with it until Kennedy come along. Then it's suddenly a national recreation area.

"So when they came to give us our assessment, this guy knocks on the door. My dad had just built a new house. This guy walks all the way through the house without stoppin', then went out the back door and turned around and said, 'Here's your assessment, Mr. Balentine.' It was take it or leave it. If you didn't take it they'd put your money in a federal bank in Hopkinsville or Paducah, and then the sheriff would come and get you, and they'd bulldoze you. It was their property now, 'cause they'd paid you for it. I knew of two instances where that happened. It was the TVA. They were the agency charged with doin' it, 'cause around here they were more powerful than the government itself. They had built all the dams, and they had all the power."

Spencer Balentine is the proprietor of the Silver Trail Distillery in Hardin, just outside the boundaries of the LBL. In an ironic twist of fate, moonshining was legalized in Kentucky in the fall

Thomas Balentine, moonshiner in Kentucky's Land Between the Lakes, with his delivery truck, and his son Spencer Balentine, proprietor of Silver Trail Distillery, posing with his dad's truck. COURTESY SPENCER BALENTINE

of 2011 (as long as you paid your taxes, of course), and Spencer has dedicated himself to re-creating and maintaining his family's heritage. In his mind the government had a powerful motive for seizing the land: revenge. The LBL had been notorious for many years as a local center of moonshining. The federal revenue agents captured a few here and there, but the moonshiners kept eluding them despite their efforts.

Many former residents share Spencer's feelings.

"Most people between the rivers had something to do with moonshine," says a woman who grew up in Golden Pond, who agreed to be interviewed but declined to be named. "It was part of life. I'd say at least half of them was involved. My uncles was both in World War II, and when they came back there was no work. After they flooded the land for Barkley Lake, that did away with a lot of the farming, so they had to find something to do.

"The TVA came in and just took everybody's land. Nobody wanted to leave, but Kennedy signed it and everybody had to go. They protested, but it didn't do any good. The TVA destroyed thousands of homes and several little towns. It's all forest land now, from the Kentucky dam all the way to the Tennessee line."

I ask her about Spencer's theory of government revenge.

"I think so too," she says. "I think the revenue men couldn't stop the moonshining, and they thought we were just a bunch of hicks. And it's true that we were very isolated, but everybody looked out for each other. They were good people—they helped each other in time of need."

The Silver Trail Distillery is located off Palestine Church Road in rural Hardin, Kentucky, on a large tract of land owned by

Spencer and his wife, Sheila. Their three-hundred-gallon copper pot still sits in an old barn, along with two smaller metal display stills made by Casey Jones, his mom's uncle and the dean of local still manufacturers. The still is running when my wife and I arrive. Spencer shows us around the barn, displaying the corn he uses for the shine—food-grade yellow corn, which has "a better taste for moonshine than white corn, more crisp." Along with that corn, he uses heavy cane syrup and a proprietary strain of yeast, although he is cagey about the exact recipe.

We move into Spencer's house and sit down at the dining room table. The living room is filled with trophies from his days as a champion motorcycle racer. He moved from there to the ownership of a Yamaha dealership but eventually—like a homing pigeon—came back to moonshine. His father, Thomas Balentine, was born in 1929 and began moonshining in 1950; Thomas's brothers were all in the business as well. Spencer tells us that his earliest childhood memory is of sitting in his dad's truck at age four or five and listening to the clunking of the glass jugs on the floor that were filled with shine.

"My dad was active from 1950 to 1959," he says. "When he was young he was a brailer, a guy who collected mussels off the riverbank, but he started moonshining after he got married. My mom hated it until the day he quit. It was the uncertainty of it, never knowing if he'd get caught and go to prison.

"They never did catch him, but they never stopped tryin'. I know that toward the end they started bringin' in ex-football players to try to run him down. One time he was runnin' and runnin, and he kept lookin' behind him and this guy was still comin'. He finally got to a creek and tripped, and his head went under. When he came up and looked back, he saw the guy had fallen over some logs.

"The closest he came to bein' caught was when him and my uncle Earl had a little still in our smokehouse. It was set up to run all winter—normally the moonshine season runs in time with the corn, but they were lookin' to extend it year-round. It was a sweet deal because my grandmother's general store was right across the road. They'd run all night, and when they got done she'd cash 'em out every mornin'.

"They did that all winter, and they were makin' more money than they ever had. But one night they were carryin' off their spent mash on the gravel road behind the house at 3:00 a.m. They're gettin' ready to dump this big barrel of mash out on the road, and then they see the local widow woman out walkin' for no reason. It was February and cold as hell, and when they saw her comin' down the road my uncle said to my dad, 'Well, we're caught.' So they got it dumped and went back. And what I remember is the next day this long green federal car pulled up in the drive, and this tall guy got out of the car and knocked on the door. He went straight from the front door to the smokehouse. When he opened it up, I remember lookin' through my dad's legs—I was 'bout five at the time—and seein' all my toys layin' over the floor, and my dad reached down to keep me quiet. So the fella looked around and said, 'Well, you got it cleaned up pretty good, didn't you?' And my dad said, 'Whatever you think.'"

Spencer hasn't stopped smiling the whole time. I ask him if his father's business was local.

"They were really a wholesale family," he says. "My great-great-grandfather would bootleg a little around Cadiz. He was what you call a whiskey artist. He'd take one of them old-time lathes or planers and chunk off big rolls of white oak. Then he'd soak it in brown sugar and water. He'd put it in a barrel of moonshine, and the stuff would be real bourbon-lookin' inside of a week." He chuckles. "He was always doin' stuff like that. He was a winemaker as well as a whiskey man. I remember when I was six he gave me my first taste of wine, and he graduated me to moonshine at seven. But of course they'd pass it off as somethin' that was good for you. They'd heat it up and put some sugar in it, and it was pretty good that way."

Actually, the smokehouse incident probably wasn't Thomas Balentine's closest call. On his website, Spencer gives a detailed account of his father's final run in 1959. On his way back, Thomas was spotted by revenue agents and pursued across the Barkley Lake bridge. He swerved off Route 68, sped down a gravel road toward Cadiz, and circled around to come home. As he approached the bridge for the second time, he saw the feds waiting for him. He rolled out of the car and watched as it careened off the bridge and into the river. As the agents searched for the car, Thomas clung to the railing underneath the bridge. It took him seven hours to get across, holding on to the underside of the bridge each time he saw headlights coming toward him. When he finally got home—shirt torn, face and hands bleeding—he looked at his wife and said two words: "That's it." He later joked that it took six minutes for a '54 Chevy to sink into the Cumberland River.

Spencer was away from moonshine for many years. After his father passed away, though, he discovered a small still on his land.

"I'd talk about it with my family and ask questions, but they'd just say, 'Naw, I'm done with that.' But what finally got me goin' was a motorcycle trip we took to Maker's Mark in June of 2009. And we got in there, and of course I hadn't been around whiskey since the 1950s. And it was exactly what I remembered—the smells, the mashin', and then the cuts, all that stuff. It all came back. As soon as I got home, I just jumped in. Once I set my mind to somethin', it's hard to stop me. I got all the paperwork, but I didn't actually get legal until 2011.

"Then I got the still built. I went up to Aurora and got all the measurements off one of my uncle's old stills. The neat thing was, my uncle knew this guy who had worked for Casey Jones when he was fifteen years old. His name was Billy Don Filbeck, and he had all the original blowtorches and soldering irons from back in the 1940s. He was eighty-four when he built my still. It took him 'bout six weeks to do it, 'cause he had to order flat pieces of copper and bend 'em by hand."

What about the recipe?

"Luckily I had a relative who had kept our recipe alive, so I had a leg up on the other distillers. When I say he kept it alive," he laughs, "I mean he put a daughter through nursing school."

As we sit there, Spencer's production is about 160 gallons daily, but he is in the process of expanding. Moonshine is booming, and when he finishes his renovations he'll have a mash room that will hold 3,500 gallons. He is also becoming a tourist destination, and has recently joined the Kentucky Bourbon Craft Trail. We begin discussing bourbon and our favorite distilleries, and he makes perhaps the most interesting observation of the day.

"What people don't realize," he says, "is that the moonshiner has it much harder to get his product right than the bourbon guys. They can mask a lot of stuff by putting it in the barrels for years. They can put the cloudy stuff in there, mix the tails in with the heads, 'cause they know the barrels will take care of the taste. We have to get the hearts out of it, it has to be clear, and we've got a much finer line than they do."

He feels strongly about perpetuating his family legacy; in fact, he admits to it being an obsession.

"I knew that if I didn't do it, it was just gonna die. If another twenty years went by and people like me were gone, nobody would know about the history of moonshine—how to do it, or where it came from, or why they did it, which was to make a livin'. Back in the fifties around here, you couldn't buy a job. Now I've got bankers who want to loan me money, but back then you couldn't get a loan on a five-hundred-acre farm. People around here were looked down on, but when they bought their homes there wasn't a single mortgage, and there were a thousand homes in LBL."

There's a knock at the back door, and we're joined at the table by Spencer's two uncles, David Balentine and Earl Crump; David is seventy-four, and Earl is well up into his eighties. They are old moonshiners from central casting, and they ease into the conversation gradually. They were in the business with Spencer's father, Thomas, and their fourth brother, Ralph, referred to as Rink. ("The standard moonshine sentence was a year and a day," Spencer tells me later, "and you usually did nine months. My uncle

Rink got caught makin' shine, so he went and did his nine months. He came back with a design for a round condenser written on hand towels, so he spent his time well.")

"I was just tellin' 'em 'bout Dad," says Spencer. "You know, when Dad made his run, he used to take the shine up to Clarksville, Tennessee. There was a black family up there that used to buy it. They'd peddle it out in pints and half-pints to the soldiers at Fort Campbell."

"Yeah," says David. "You'd drive into an underground garage, and two of the sons would unload 150 or 200 gallons for you. Then the woman would pay you off in a paper sack, the third son would open the back door, and you'd drive out. It all took 'bout five minutes."

"So one night," recalls Spencer, "my dad made a run up there with a friend of his, and when they got there they were the last car—there'd been 'bout five ahead of them. The woman had run out of bills, so she gave them silver. The next morning they went up to the garage where they were havin' some work done on one of their cars. They went to pay the bill, which was around $95. They got all the silver out and started countin' it, and the garage boys jumped up and said, 'You're the sons of bitches who robbed the Dover bank last night!' They figured my dad and his friend just had to be the bank robbers, because why else would they have all that silver? So those guys always thought of him as a bank robber rather than a moonshiner, and of course he could never tell them where the money actually come from."

"Yeah," laughs David, "those boys thought your daddy was a bank robber till the day they died."

I ask Earl about his career in the business.

"I was never much of a moonshiner," he says. "But I was laid off one winter and Tommy, Spencer's daddy, said why don't you help me back up some barrels? I said no, I never did go for that, but I ended up workin' with him in the smokehouse. Tommy had all the equipment, the cooker and such, so all we needed was the sugar and the corn. So we set up four barrels in the smokehouse, and we could do them four barrels from dark to daylight. So we added four more, and then we added four more. Then we could work all night seven nights a week and make a bunch of whiskey."

He laughs and tells the story of being discovered dumping the mash at three in the morning, and of the federal agent who came to bust them and found nothing but little Spencer's toys on the floor of the smokehouse.

"But we had a good long run. The still ran slow and took a long time, but it had a good turnout. But that was about the extent of it for me. I hauled a little here and there, but I was never really a moonshiner. I went back to work somewhere after that. I always tried to have a job—I thought a lot about that penitentiary. And after that I actually worked at the prison for five years, and I knew I didn't want to end up there."

I ask him how many stills there were in the area when he was making shine in the smokehouse.

"Well, back then you'd get five gallons of whiskey off one barrel of beer [distiller's beer, or low wine]. But one day me and another guy sat out on the porch of the service station and counted up 3,500 gallons that we knew about, that were leavin' the land between the rivers every five or six days. That's a bunch of barrels."

"This Bogard guy that was so active in the late twenties," says Spencer, "he was the one that had the three shifts runnin', wasn't he? He had three big shifts and two crews workin' for him. He had his own labels and everything."

"Yeah, he was a big operator," says Earl. "Joe Bogard. He was big at that time."

According to LBL lore, Joe Bogard's boys used to take the shine out into the cornfields at night, armed with lanterns. Al Capone's planes used to land, pick it up, and take it to Chicago.

"He wasn't as big as some guys was," says David. "John Allen Lloyd, he ran 175 barrels at a time, back when he had his big still made. Had it made at a machine shop in Hopkinsville. He had it delivered, but never got it to the place. The revenue men caught it and they tried to chop it up. When that didn't work," he chuckles, "they tried to blow it up. But they found out who made it. They went up to Hopkinsville, and the shop told them it was made for John Allen Lloyd. So he went to the penitentiary for that."

Unlike Earl, David was full-time in the business.

"It was a lot of hard work," he says. "When you take a hundred pounds of sugar on your shoulder and five gallons of gas in your hand, and go a quarter-mile with it, it wasn't easy. But everybody had their job."

"The worst job was the water guy," adds Spencer. "Those old condensers, of course, they didn't have runnin' water into 'em, and they had these wooden plugs. When they got heated up somebody would pull the plug, and somebody else would have to go down to the creek and put the water back into it."

"We had to keep movin' the stills around," says David, "dependin' on the water. I guess the longest we stayed in one place was eighteen months. It was a quarter-mile up a big hill and down the other side of the hill. Things would get so bad around the water holes that we'd have to load the barrels into the truck and drive them back into the woods to sit for five days. We'd take some leaves and pat 'em down, and they'd never find 'em.

"And you were scared to death. You were always lookin' over your shoulder. The first two federal men over there were John Bays and Dewey Harrison. You could track Harrison through the woods 'cause he ate boiled eggs, and he'd leave a track of shells. Bays, he smoked Camel cigarettes. You'd always know when he'd been in the area, 'cause he'd twist the butts out with his foot against the leaves. You'd have to be sharp, and fast on your feet. Spencer's dad, he could hear a stick break from a quarter-mile away."

"We didn't worry 'bout no local law or county law," says Earl. "It was the revenue men that you had to worry 'bout."

"Yeah," says David, "the federal men got really bad. They brought in three other guys that was former football players."

"Those were the ones that tried to run daddy down," says Spencer.

"We didn't have no fast cars, neither," says David. "We'd haul two hundred gallons up to Clarksville in a '49 Plymouth coupe. We had rubber boots under the springs. We'd load the car up and then blow the boots up until the car sat level. You always needed a woman to sit in the passenger seat, so it didn't look like you were haulin' shine. Back then, if they caught you, they'd charge you for anything—they didn't care about the amount."

Sheila asks how much money they were making.

"Well, it cost 'bout a dollar and a quarter to make a gallon, and we got four dollars a gallon for it. We tried to make $100 per week apiece" [the equivalent of about $850 today].

"I have a really stupid question for you," I tell David. "There's a lot of nostalgia for that period, and some people even look back on it as romantic. Do you think people are better off now?"

"Definitely," he says. "Back then, if you went to look for a job and they asked you where you lived, and you said Golden Pond or between the rivers, that ended the interview right there. They thought we were all ignorant hillbillies, I guess. They wasn't smart enough to come up with the idea of makin' whiskey to make a livin'. But it was hard times back then." He smiles. "I was thinkin' just a while ago, when I was puttin' on my shorts and T-shirt to come over here, 'bout how you could never wear shorts when you was makin' whiskey. You had to have somethin' on so the briars wouldn't get you, and you might have to run."

"So tell me," I ask, "these federal agents—were they all on the up and up? None of them were taking bribes?"

"Naw," he grins, "they just wouldn't take 'em. None of 'em had any common sense."

"Somebody always saw the federal men comin'," says Earl.

"Oh yeah," agrees David. "You knew what kind of cars they drove. If they came in between the rivers, it didn't make no difference which way they came in—somebody would see 'em, and word would get around. If we'd had cell phones back then, they never could have gotten in at all."

"So," I ask him, "what did you do when you finally quit moonshining?"

"I worked in Detroit for a while, and then I came back and became sheriff of Callaway County."

I stare at him in disbelief.

"Yep," says Spencer, "a state trooper asked him one time, how can you find these guys? And I'll never forget his answer: You got to be tracked, to be able to track."

I suggest to Spencer that maybe it's time to taste some moonshine. He disappears into the kitchen and comes back with bottles and shot glasses. He pours a taste of his flagship whiskey, LBL Moonshine. The nose is filled with whiffs of sweet corn and heady alcohol notes (it's 100 proof, after all). It's concentrated and potent on the palate, ripe and forceful—an outstanding moonshine, and a beautiful sipping whiskey. Spencer then pours us samples of two products currently in development: his Apple Pie and Pineapple moonshine.

To my astonishment, my wife falls in love with the Apple Pie. "This is wonderful," she gushes. "I could easily have a glass of this and sip on it all night." My amazement is now boundless: This is a woman who normally refuses to drink anything other than New Zealand Sauvignon Blanc or Columbia Valley Chardonnay. Moonshine, it appears, is truly the great leveler.

Sheila comes forward and puts her arms around Spencer.

"When he told me what he was going to do," she says, "I thought we would never succeed. But I'm proud of him that he's re-creating his family heritage. It's been really interesting to have people from between the rivers come and visit us. They just go into the distillery and smell the smells, and tears come to their eyes.

"I just want to say one thing," she says. "People think that this moonshine revival is a trend, but it's really an American love affair. You either love it or you hate it." She smiles. "Most people, they just love it."

RECIPES
Courtesy of Spencer Balentine

LBL Moonshine Sunset Inn

The Sunset Inn was the hot spot for food and drink between the rivers in the 1940s and '50s. Spencer says his father lost many a paycheck to the slot machines in the back.

> **1½ ounces 100-proof LBL Moonshine**
> **4 ounces Sunny D orange drink**
> **¼ ounce pomegranate syrup**
> **Orange or lime wedge, for garnish**

Mix over ice cubes in a rocks glass; garnish with an orange or lime wedge.

LBL Moonshine Brushcutter

The Brushcutters were a hardy breed of men in the early 1950s who wielded axes and handsaws, clearing the rugged undergrowth for what is now the Trace Highway through the LBL. Most of these laborers' weekends were spent sampling the local moonshine and chasing the local LBL girls.

    1½ ounces 100-proof LBL moonshine
    4 ounces strawberry margarita mix
    Lime wedge, for garnish

Pour over crushed ice and top off with a lime wedge.

LBL Moonshine Apple Toss

    2 ounces 100-proof LBL Moonshine
    1 ounce apple juice
    1 ounce apple cider
    Dash of vanilla extract
    1 teaspoon brown sugar
    Cinnamon stick, for garnish (optional)

Combine ingredients in a shaker, shake, and serve over ice. Garnish with a cinnamon stick if desired.

MB ROLAND

Paul and Merry Beth Tomaszewski are not typical moonshiners. They aren't descended from generations of outlaws who made illegal liquor up in the hills, so moonshine is not in their DNA. They fit none of the colorful stereotypes we have come to expect: They are a hardworking, well-scrubbed young couple who were not involved in the liquor industry prior to getting their license in 2009.

Spend some time with Paul Tomaszewski, however, and you'll realize that he is an exceptionally talented distiller who just happens to be making moonshine.

Their distillery, MB Roland, is located in the small town of Saint Elmo, Kentucky, just outside Pembroke in Christian County. The sprawling property is a former Amish dairy farm. The barn has been repurposed to make whiskey, and there is a small shed for smoking corn. The nerve center of the operation is a building that serves as a gift shop, tasting room, kitchen, and office.

Paul is from Pearl River, Louisiana, a little town near New Orleans—"the land of the drive-through daiquiri hut," as he jokingly refers to it, although he was never much of a drinker. He joined the army after high school and graduated from West Point; his five years as an officer included two tours of duty in Iraq. "It motivates you very quickly into one of two camps," he observes. "Either you're going to stay in the army for the long haul, or you're going to get out. I don't miss it on a lot of levels, but it set the foundation for a lot of my future life."

After his second deployment in Iraq, he was stationed at Fort Campbell, Kentucky, and was introduced to Scotch whiskey by his older brother. "It was fun to try," he says, "and it was interesting. At the time I really didn't have a hobby—I had been moving around constantly and needed to keep my possessions to a minimum. But by the time I finished my second deployment, I could lead a normal life, and I got really interested in whiskey and distilling."

Something else was brewing in his life. He had met and married Merry Beth Roland, and the couple wanted to start a business.

"So here we were in Kentucky, and you could hop in the car and tour some of the world's greatest distilleries within a few hours. And as I started researching the market, I stumbled on some micro-distilleries, which was a totally new and fascinating concept. It almost started as a dare to myself, just to see how things would turn out, without having any real intention of developing this into a business."

"When we started," says Merry Beth, "we were slightly underfunded. But then this property came up for sale, and it just

True Kentucky Shine, distilled and bottled at MB Roland Distillery in Kentucky. COURTESY MB ROLAND DISTILLERY

wasn't something you could pass up. I knew Paul could do it—he has the personality, and you can't stop him once he puts his mind to something. The question was, did we want to put everything we owned into it?"

"We thought it was perfect," adds Paul. "We were near the interstate, and we were in a wet county—the only one in the area. So the bank believed us, and here we are, almost making a living. Of course," he laughs, "I still drive a Honda Civic with 150,000 miles on it, and it'll stay that way for a while. But we're on the right path."

Merry Beth grew up in Robertson County, Tennessee, about twenty-five miles from where we're sitting. I ask her if she had moonshining in her family.

"Oh, no!" she exclaims. "We didn't even drink. I came from a family of teetotalers."

"That's one difference between here and Louisiana," laughs Paul. "Around here, if people tell you they don't drink, they really don't drink. When they tell you they don't drink in Louisiana, it means they only drink socially. Liquor is just a part of Louisiana culture—you find it at every occasion and family get-together."

I wonder if, coming from a background of nondrinking Southerners, if moonshine carried any stigma for her.

"Well, yes," she says. "But our intent was never just to do moonshine. We really see ourselves as a bourbon distillery, a place that is utilizing something else out there with the background and reference point to get us where we want to go. Our intent was always to make bourbon. I mean, you can't be a Kentucky distillery and not make bourbon."

In fact, very near the barn where the distilling takes place, the Tomaszewskis have a rick house in waiting, a building with natural climate control that will be perfect for the aging of bourbon. And while they do have some barrels in there, they are currently very far from being a bourbon distillery. The reality is that their financial hardships would have been far worse if they had committed to making only bourbon: They would have been sitting around staring at barrels for six or seven years before they made a dime.

I ask them if they received any inspiration or guidance in the making of corn whiskey from old-time moonshiners.

"There were a couple of locals who provided a lot of historical background," says Paul. "There's a gentleman named William Turner, who's up in his eighties now, who knows everything about Christian County and then some. He's the local historian. And there was another gentleman in Cadiz named Bucky Oliver that I talked to, and he actually made shine back in the '70s, when most counties were dry. That was the thing about this area that I came to understand—you had a cluster of dry counties, so people had to drive hours to buy any alcohol legally. That's the reason that moonshine flourished. To this day, in dry counties that I won't mention, you'll have ad hoc liquor stores behind people's homes. And still, nobody seems to get the idea that the system doesn't work."

"Once people found out what we were doing," says Merry Beth, "they would come by our place and talk to us. They'd impart quite a bit of knowledge. But sometimes I'd feel like saying, 'You do realize that everything you just told me is illegal?'

"We get calls from people all the time that have been making shine for years, and they're just contemplating the idea of going legal. When someone stops by, you can always tell if they're making it, or if they used to make it. The only thing they want to do is see your still. Then they want to taste it, to see how it compares to what they've made. I think a lot of people come out here to make comparisons, but they also end up sharing their story."

"Things have changed a lot just in the last few years," says Paul. "When we first had visitors, if they were consumers, it was a lot more explanatory. We'd have to educate people about exactly

Paul and Merry Beth Tomaszewski, owners of MB Roland Distillery, put the finishing touches on a barrel. COURTESY MB ROLAND DISTILLERY

what we were doing. Now people will show up, and they get the fact that it's moonshine. If you want to taste something that has the flavor of what it used to be, this is it—without getting in trouble, of course."

In fact, things have changed to the point where the Tomaszewskis, after barely five years in the business, are now old-timers and role models themselves. Several times each year, they teach a course called Camp Distillery, an intensive program that takes would-be entrepreneurs through all the details and nuances of starting a business.

"When we decided to go down this road," recalls Paul, "I did a lot of research, and eventually realized there just wasn't a bunch of information out there about how to do it. You can't really go to college to learn how to be a distiller. And if you work at a big distillery, that experience really doesn't translate into an operation our size. Then there's the whole marketing side. In a perfect world, if you're doing a start-up, you really need someone who knows the production side, and also someone who knows the marketing and sales end of the business. So we try to share all of that with people, and the course is sold out every time."

"We had a lot of folks knocking on our door, wanting to pick our brains," says Merry Beth. "There aren't a lot of resources out there for people who want to start this business, and we couldn't stop and explain everything to each one individually, so we developed this course. And hopefully it helps them avoid some of the pitfalls we went through. We didn't have the funds to hire a marketing person, but that worked in our favor—we had to learn everything that we needed to do, and not depend on anyone else."

The learning curve may have been steep, but it's been effective. In addition to running the gift shop and teaching Camp Distillery, the Tomaszewskis sponsor an event called Pickin' on the Porch. Every two weeks from May to November, country bands serenade visitors on the porch of the building; there are food vendors, beer, snow cones—and, of course, moonshine. These events have become widely popular and attract nearly a thousand locals to the distillery each time. In addition, Paul and Merry Beth are founding members of the Kentucky Bourbon Trail Craft Tour, founded in conjunction with the Kentucky Distillers Association—a group that includes their friend Spencer Balentine, who also mentored them in the beginning.

I ask them why they think that moonshine has become such a trend, not just in the South but nationally.

"Personally," says Merry Beth, "I think it's just the state of America right now. Everyone is fascinated with Southern culture. TV has a lot to do with it. It has a lot of impact on people."

"The entertainment industry always seems to go after the South," says Paul. "But there are two sides to it. Growing up in Louisiana, as I told you, liquor was such a part of the culture that there was no need for moonshine. So when I came up here, I wanted to try it. It was something I had always heard about, and I think a lot of people have that kind of attitude toward our products. But a lot of the interest comes from the hullabaloo of television, which makes it tough for us. We're trying to run an honest business in a professional manner, and TV makes it look like a joke."

Is it really a joke, I wonder, or do those stories just look sexy to people leading boring lives? I ask them if it embarrasses them, as Southerners, when they see shows like *Moonshiners* on TV?

"Some of it does," admits Merry Beth. "The true South, and the genteel aspect of things that I grew up with, just isn't being represented very well. I understand it, but I don't agree with a lot of it."

"You have people who are rough around the edges," says Paul, "no matter whether you're in Kentucky or California or Brooklyn. And sometimes the way they're portrayed is less than favorable. If you don't know that person on an individual basis, you think all Southerners are like that."

"Right," laughs Merry Beth. "For example, we wear shoes."

"There are things in every state that people aren't proud of, or may not agree with," says Paul. "But the public perception is going to depend on the way it's portrayed. Here's a case in point. When the production company that actually did the *Moonshiners* show was looking for subject matter, they came and visited us. And I basically told them that we weren't going to act like we were out in the woods doing this illegally. You could tell the direction they were going in. But they had no interest in covering a distillery that was doing things legally—they wanted to dumb it down."

"It's just a sign of the times," agrees Merry Beth. "When I was growing up, if someone said something impolite, you just turned your back and ignored it. We're not that way anymore. It's a circus now. If someone happens to do something that's inappropriate, other people are waiting to exploit it. There are some things in every state that people aren't proud of. I just wish that more effort was made not to make some folks appear quite as ridiculous as they do sometimes."

At this point I suggest that we taste some moonshine, and we retreat to the tasting bar. Paul pulls out a formidable array of products. Their True Kentucky Shine (100 proof, 50 percent alcohol by volume) has a floral nose with fragrant aromas of citrus and apples. It is sweet on entry, turning spicy in the mid-palate, with a long, resonant finish. We follow this with their Kentucky White Dog and Kentucky Black Dog. The Black Dog is particularly fascinating—made from white corn smoked on the premises, it has an intriguing barbecue flavor to it. There's also Blackberry Shine, Pink Lemonade, and Apple Pie.

"We make everything from scratch," says Paul, "and we made a point from the beginning to do that. There are a lot of folks out there that are taking shortcuts. The easy way to explain it is that their money goes into marketing, and ours goes into the product. We're selling ours for the same price, but I know that it costs a lot more to make, because we're producing it authentically. There are people that are using GNS [grain neutral spirits]. If you're just going to make vodka that has no color or flavor to it, I guess you might as well buy it. But we said, let's make a distinctive product. It may be a clear whiskey, but it needs to have flavor to it. The shine is distilled so that it comes off the still at 125 proof, not 180 proof, and has distinctive corn flavor. And if you talk to the old-time moonshiners, they made it the same way."

"We wanted to be authentic," adds Merry Beth. "When we committed to doing this, we wanted to do it in a manner that would be representative of what you would have historically found. We were just going to do it legally and better."

I may be here to taste moonshine, and I have, but I'm itching to try that bourbon. I convince Paul to go out to the rick house and pull a barrel sample for me. It is absolutely amazing—full-bodied, rich and powerful, but elegant and graceful at the same time. It comes in at 106 proof, 53 percent alcohol by volume, without a trace of heat. In fact, it compares favorably to some of the more celebrated and expensive small-batch bourbons on the market. The only problem is that there isn't enough of it—yet. I'm intrigued with where they think they'll be in five years' time.

"I believe we'll end up being a combination of two distillers in one," says Merry Beth. "Some people come out here looking specifically for bourbon, and that's why we got into the business. And of course there are other folks who could just care less."

"We're in the process of expanding our operation," agrees Paul. "We've gotten the green light from the banks, and we'll be producing a lot more whiskey in the years to come. As we increase production, we'd like to tilt a bit toward aged spirits. But that's not always going to work out, because you have to sell what people want."

In fact, Paul is already spending more time on the road, riding around in cars with distributor salespeople, doing the hard work of promoting his product one account at a time. For the moment, that product is moonshine. When the time comes that MB Roland is capitalized well enough to make and age more bourbon—watch out.

RECIPES
Courtesy of MB Roland

Thin Mintini

1 part MB Roland True Kentucky Shine
1 part white crème de cacao
½ part crème de menthe

Combine ingredients in a shaker over ice; shake and strain into a martini glass.

Self-Diagnosis

1 part MB Roland True Kentucky Shine
1½ parts Dr. Pepper
1½ parts vanilla cream soda

Combine ingredients and serve in rocks glass over ice.

Milk Chocolate Elmo

1 ounce MB Roland St. Elmo's Fire
½ ounce Bailey's Irish Cream
¾ ounce Kahlua
1 ounce Godiva chocolate liqueur
Splash of half and half

Combine ingredients in a shaker over ice; shake well and strain into rocks glass.

Apple Pie Manhattan

3 parts MB Roland Apple Pie Kentucky Shine
1 part MB Roland True Kentucky Shine
¼ part sweet vermouth
Cherry, apple slice, cinnamon stick, or ground cinnamon, for garnish

Combine ingredients in a shaker over ice; shake well and strain into a cocktail glass. Garnish with cherry, apple slice, and cinnamon stick and/or sprinkle of cinnamon powder.

Kentucky Fireball

2 parts MB Roland True Kentucky Shine
1 part DeKuyper Hot Damn cinnamon liqueur

Combine ingredients in a shaker over ice; strain into rocks glass.

Sandy's Apple Pie Shine Bread Pudding

Courtesy of Sandy Tomaszewski, Paul's mother, currently living in their home town of Pearl River, Louisiana

For the pudding:
1 loaf day-old French bread
1 quart milk (approximate)
3 eggs, slightly beaten
1 to 1½ cups sugar

2 tablespoons vanilla extract

¼ teaspoon cinnamon

(Sometimes I get wild and throw in a bit of nutmeg and/or allspice)

1–2 large cooking apples, peeled and chopped

3 tablespoons melted butter

(If you opt to add raisins, soaking them in shine for a while is recommended. Also, pecans are an additional tasty option.)

Soak bread in milk in a large bowl for at least an hour. Preheat oven to 350°F. Crush bread with your hands until bread is mixed well with milk. Add eggs, sugar, vanilla, cinnamon, spices, apples, and butter. Stir well.

Pour batter into the bottom of a thick, ovenproof 9 x 13-inch glass casserole and bake until firm (35–45 minutes) in a shallow pan of warm water. You can test with a toothpick. Cool, then cube into servings. For extra flair, put under the broiler for 2–3 minutes. Serve with MB Roland's Apple Pie Kentucky Shine Sauce!

MB Roland's Apple Pie Kentucky Shine Sauce

1 cup sugar

½ cup (1 stick) butter

1 egg, well beaten

MB Roland Apple Pie Kentucky Shine

Cook sugar and butter until well dissolved. Gradually whisk beaten egg into cooled sauce mixture (so as not to cook/curdle egg); stir constantly, and take care not to brown the butter. Set aside until cooled. Add MB Roland Apple Pie Kentucky Shine to taste. Note: I always double the sauce, and I'm quite generous with the shine!

MB's Kentucky Pink Lemonade Cupcakes

Delicious and decadent—courtesy of Merry Beth Tomaszewski

For the cupcakes:

1½ cups all-purpose flour
¾ cup sugar
2 teaspoons baking powder
½ tsp. salt
½ cup (1 stick) butter (room temperature)
½ cup light sour cream (room temperature)
2 large eggs (room temperature)
2 teaspoons vanilla extract
¼ cup MB Roland Kentucky Pink Lemonade

For the buttercream frosting:

¾ cup (1½ sticks) butter (room temperature)
3 ounces light cream cheese (room temperature)
1 teaspoon vanilla extract
½ cup MB Roland Kentucky Pink Lemonade
¼ cup MB Roland Kentucky Strawberry Shine
8 cups powdered sugar

Preheat oven to 350°F. Line muffin/cupcake tin (12-cupcake capacity) with paper cups. Whisk flour, sugar, baking powder, and salt together. Add butter, sour cream, eggs, and vanilla. Beat with an electric mixer on medium speed until smooth and silky, about 1 minute. Divide batter evenly among cupcake cups and bake approximately 20–25 minutes. Cupcake tops will be a pale gold, and a toothpick inserted into the center should come out clean. Remove cupcakes from tin and cool to room temperature before frosting.

For the frosting, mix the butter and cream cheese on medium-high speed for 2–3 minutes. Add the vanilla, Kentucky Pink Lemonade, Kentucky Strawberry Shine, and powdered sugar. Beat until light and fluffy. If the icing is too thick, add more of the Kentucky Pink Lemonade. If it's too thin, add more powdered sugar. This recipe makes enough for 24 cupcakes.

The recipe is easily altered to suit your tastes, such as adding chopped strawberries, lemon zest, or even topping with coconut. It's fun and delicious, though for adults only, as the alcohol content only cooks off in the cupcake batter. It's still very much present in the frosting.

☆ ☆ ☆

TROY & SONS

Troy Ball has been called a force of nature, but that description is an understatement. Spend some time with her, and you quickly realize that she could probably move mountains—calmly, cheerfully, and gracefully, with someone standing on the peaks not realizing they had budged an inch. Her distillery, Troy & Sons, is located in an industrial area outside the city of Asheville, next to the Highland Brewing Company. While the facility is large, modern, and easily accessible to tourists, Troy's journey to get there was a convoluted one.

It goes without saying that she is a woman in a man's world. While there have been many female distillers over the past two centuries, and it's now almost common to find them in Scotland, female moonshiners are rare. This is ironic when you consider the historical role that women played in the production of moonshine: They had to be ready to step in when their husbands were arrested and sent to prison, which occurred frequently. If you were the wife

Troy Ball, modern female moonshiner and proprietor of Troy & Sons in Asheville, North Carolina. COURTESY TROY & SONS DISTILLERY

of a moonshiner, being knowledgeable and adept at the operation of the still often determined whether or not your family survived. When the husbands were released from jail, however, the wives tended to fade into the background once again.

Troy's success in the world of moonshine is closely related to her own family story. As the parent of two special-needs sons, both nonverbal and confined to wheelchairs, she had to develop perseverance early on. Marshall, the oldest, communicates with an alphabet board and has published two books, largely with the help of his mother. Coulton refused food from his infant years and had to be fed from an eyedropper, a process that sometimes took the better part of a day. Not the experience of an average soccer mom, to be sure, but certainly an endeavor that inspires a person to shrug off the impossible.

After graduating from Vanderbilt with a degree in marketing and business, she met and married her husband, Charlie, a civil engineer who did commercial real estate development. The couple lived in Texas, where Troy was consumed with giving twenty-four-hour care to her two sons. They moved to North Carolina in 2003 in search of a better environment for their children—a place "with a true winter, rather than allergy season on top of allergy season." She admits that their goal in moving was simply to keep the kids alive, and that they had no idea what they would do. The Balls purchased several large tracts of land in Madison County and began to settle into their new home.

And then a strange thing happened. As they met and became friendly with the locals, the old-timers started bringing them moonshine.

"That was their way of telling you that they liked you," she says. "It's the custom, and they think it's fun. So we had a lot of illegal moonshine delivered to us that way, and it was awful—it was always hot, and it got to the point where I would just smell it, then put the lid back on and stash it under the stairs. And finally, one day an old railway sheriff told me that the good stuff never leaves the home place. They'd keep it and drink it, and give away the junk.

"One day in 2008 he showed up at my house and said he had something special for me. I said, if it's moonshine I don't want it," she laughs. "And he said no, this was the good stuff, and I promised him I'd try it.

"My sister came over later that afternoon and I told her about the moonshine. She tasted it and said it was definitely different. Then I tasted it, and I was pleasantly surprised—I never had been a hard-liquor drinker. Later that night I had a group of women coming over, and I asked them if they wanted to try some moonshine. We mixed it with fruit juice, and they drank the entire jar."

It was her first experience with keeper moonshine—the kind that the old-timers stashed away for themselves.

"The next morning, I woke up wondering if you could actually make that kind of white whiskey. I went to the store and bought all the products available back in 2008, and none of them tasted like the stuff he brought me. And I thought, why aren't we making quality American whiskey? What's holding us back? So I went back to the sheriff and told him that I wanted to learn how to make moonshine, if one of his friends would teach me. He told me I was nuts, of course, that they would never even talk to me."

Thus began Troy Ball's romance with a group that she refers to as "the old guys"—classic moonshiners who mentored her in the art of producing first-class American corn whiskey.

"I'd say it took about four or five months before he actually found someone who was willing to have me observe the process," she recalls. "And after I saw it, I realized it wasn't all that complicated. But what I saw over time was that the guys who were making whiskey to keep for themselves knew a lot about where the sweet spot was in the distillation process, and that's the part they kept."

She's referring, of course, to the hearts. But could it really be as simple as isolating the hearts from the acetone- and aldehyde-infused heads, or the flabby and undistinguished tails? She had a lot to learn, but she was aided in her quest by the fact that she had grown up on a farm—despite her elegant appearance, Troy Ball is a woman who is just as comfortable on a tractor as she would be at a debutante ball. As she gradually made friends with the moonshiners who made some of the best whiskey around, things began to come into focus.

"The old guys thought it was funny," she says, "but they eventually realized that I was serious about learning how to do it. I think they appreciated the fact that I would show up day after day, work as hard as I did and get as dirty as I had to get. And it turned out that the ones who made the really good whiskey did it the same way we're doing it here. They discarded the first 10 percent of the run—the heads—separated the hearts, and also separated the last 30 percent of tails. That 60 percent of pure hearts was the keeper moonshine they drank themselves. I had a guy who showed up here one day, and he pulled me aside after the tour and said, 'Troy, the way you're making whiskey here is exactly what we used to do in Madison County.' This guy had a fifty-gallon still. When the whiskey started smelling sweet and all the acetone was gone, he'd collect twelve quart jars. They'd take the heads and the tails, mix them together and sell them up the road. Those twelve quart jars were the ones they kept."

And what did her husband think about all this?

"He thought I had gone totally crazy," she laughs. "But in my mind, I knew I had been waiting a long time to go into my own business. I think learning about the process, and coming down here and stabilizing my children, made me realize that the time had come. So I bought a five-gallon pressure cooker and badgered him into helping me modify it into a still. I remember the day we went to Lowe's to buy parts for the still—the men who worked there were laughing their heads off. They told us, 'We're not even going to ask you what you intend to do with this stuff.' This was in 2010, and I had spent almost two years trying to learn the craft from the old guys.

"Then I needed to find the corn. I noticed that everyone who was making good whiskey used white corn. I went over to the University of Tennessee and talked to a corn scientist, and he explained to me that historically, people ate white corn and fed yellow corn to their animals. So up in the mountains where it's hard to find tillable land, you'll use whatever land you have to grow white corn your family can eat.

"I asked around, and everybody told me to contact John McEntire at Peaceful Valley Farm, on Crooked Creek. I called him and told him I wanted to buy some corn. He asked me how much, and when I told him a hundred pounds he said, 'Are you that lady that wants to make whiskey?' When I went out to the farm to talk to him, he told me about the Crooked Creek Corn. This was an old variety that had been cultivated on the property since the 1800s, and multiple families used to grow it. The McEntires were the last ones, and many people assumed it was extinct. When I showed it to the corn expert at the University of Tennessee, he ran an analysis on it and said he had never seen anything like it—the fat content was much higher, for one thing. But that was

Farmer John McEntire, who grows the heirloom Crooked Creek Corn for Troy & Sons. COURTESY TROY & SONS DISTILLERY

Moonshine Nation

the type of corn that was always grown, at least until Monsanto came along.

"John agreed to sell me the corn and help me get started, provided I got a federal permit. We got the permit in the fall of 2010 and spent the next year doing trial distillations on John's farm. A friend of his helped us build a whiskey barrel still with a hundred-gallon pot. The thing that was fantastic about that still was that the distillate came off with an oaked flavor, and that's eventually how we developed our Troy & Sons Oak Reserve. I kept logs on everything, and the guys really got a charge out of me. We finally released our first product to the public in August 2011."

"Troy is a vibrant, energetic person," says John McEntire when I contact him by phone. "It's just been a world of fun working with her and watching this project evolve."

I ask him what was so special about Crooked Creek Corn, from his point of view.

"It used to be commonplace to this area," he says. "This was a small, agrarian region, and a hundred years back everyone grew it. Every small community had their own mill, and they'd grind it up to make cornbread and grits—and moonshine, of course, although it wasn't usually talked about. But most everybody around here had a small still on their property. People made moonshine for their own consumption, for medicinal purposes, or to supplement their income.

"Crooked Creek Corn started dying out when supermarkets and large milling operations began selling cornmeal. It was easier for people to grind it than to grow it themselves. My family was unique in that we kept on growing it. It's an open-pollinated field corn, an heirloom variety. It's not a hybrid, totally non-GMO. We've been very careful not to plant it in fields next to ones that grow GMO corn."

I ask him what being involved with Troy & Sons has meant to him.

"It's been a way to help protect the heritage of this area. The corn is just one example. My father and grandfather loved cornbread, and they had a little stone mill on the property. After my parents passed away, we started giving tours of the farm to local schoolkids. Over time, I realized that one of the things they liked the most was seeing the mill in operation.

"Appalachian mountain people were unique in many ways— independent and self-sufficient. That's part of the tradition in these mountains that's important, that needs to be preserved. It's interesting to me that many of our founding fathers had stills, and it wasn't frowned upon back then. When the temperance movement started, though, it went underground. However people perceive that history, there's a myth to it that's intriguing and should be remembered."

Back at the distillery, Troy pours some moonshine for us to taste. The Troy & Sons Platinum ($31) displays fragrant corn aromas on the nose, as well as a firm core of sweet corn on the palate; expressive, compact, and flavorful, it finishes long and spicy. The Oak Reserve ($37), aged in used bourbon barrels, has a pale tan color, and hints of honey and vanilla mixed in with corn scents on the nose. It's more forceful and spicy in the mouth than the Platinum, with fresh herbs and pepper in the mid-palate leading to a graceful finish. Aged in new, charred American white oak barrels, the Blonde Whiskey ($43) exhibits a nose of vanilla and sweet caramel. It is soft, mellow, and nuanced, and the rich mid-palate is marked by a nice balance between corn, oak, and spice—an impressive whiskey.

"We decided from the beginning that we wanted to be ultra-premium and authentic," she says. "That's why we call it Heirloom Moonshine. White whiskey in America is an original product—if you were making whiskey in America two hundred years ago, that's what you were making."

I ask her about a reference on her website to Bishop Asbury, a preacher in western North Carolina.

"I went down to the North Carolina State Archives and pulled out everything on whiskey, moonshine, styles of distillation, all the old information I could find. And I found out that the old circuit-riding preachers usually carried moonshine around with them. That's how they tended their flock. They called it blockade whiskey, or white liquor. What I was trying to do was bring products to the market that were reminiscent of those early whiskeys.

"I think it's important for people to understand the early history of whiskey production in America—not just Prohibition, which everybody seems to be stuck on. During Prohibition, you started getting more poorly made spirits. Before that, people weren't under any pressure. They made the whiskey they wanted to make, and they took their time making it. But Prohibition changed that, and it also made it possible for unscrupulous distillers to get away with products that were actually harmful to people, in some cases."

I mention Spencer Balentine's theory that producers of aged whiskey have it much easier, because they can put the heads and tails into the barrels with the knowledge that they'll be absorbed over time.

"I think that's true. The barrels really do mask a lot. And I suspect that's one reason why they age their whiskey as long as they do. Over time, you also get that 30 percent evaporation—what some folks call the angel's share—and there's a greater chance that the acetones and aldehydes will come off, or at least dissipate. So of course the whiskey gets cleaner when you let it sit around for six years. But if you put clear hearts whiskey in a barrel and age it, you have a really soft whiskey right from the beginning."

We walk out into the actual distillery area. The equipment is mostly new and extremely high-tech, but the space is dominated by one particular piece: an enormous, gleaming copper pot still. It's capable of holding five thousand liters and was manufactured by Kothe, Europe's leading still maker. The still was designed by Troy's husband, Charlie, who has cheerfully made the transition to being a legal moonshiner, and who traveled to Germany to supervise the construction. I ask her how they make use of all this technology without allowing the technology to take control of the process.

"Well, we don't have the system automated. The computers monitor everything, but we insist on making the cuts ourselves, using our noses. There's a pattern to it, and over time we were able to observe the exact temperatures at which we were making the cuts, but we still do it manually. Every fermentation is slightly different, so we're not about to turn the entire process over to the computers."

She pauses for a moment.

"You know, it's possible to hugely increase the amount of hearts simply by adjusting the temperature. We typically get about two hundred gallons per run. One day early on, when the equipment was new, we suddenly discovered that we had more than three hundred gallons, and the quality of the distillate had changed. Instead of all the distinctive fruit aromas we normally get, it was duller and flatter. And it turned out that the system had automatically adjusted the temperature by five degrees. Since then we do everything manually, but it gives you an idea of how some distillers can increase production at the cost of quality.

"We decided to make a product that we love, and we're giving up a lot to do that—basically, we're sacrificing 40 percent of the distillate. We don't combine the heads and tails and then redistill them, which is what most folks do. When you start learning about the different ways you can cut corners, it's very tempting, because it's so expensive to make everything from scratch."

The current annual production at Troy & Sons is around twenty-five thousand six-bottle cases, but that imposing Kothe still has the capability to boost the number to one hundred thousand eventually. When that happens, perhaps in five years, Troy will fulfill her goal of becoming a national brand; currently, the product is distributed in ten states.

"As we grow," she says, "we want to remain a real brand and not become a tourist brand. Right now, the risk with the whole moonshine category is that there are so many bad products out there that are tainting the opportunity for moonshine. And of course there are people who are really making vodka and passing it off as moonshine, which works because it's much softer.

Consumers are really curious about moonshine and want to try it, but if they get a bad bottle they won't buy it twice.

"When I got the idea to do this, I was influenced by some of Ross Perot's early messaging. He said that in order to succeed, you had to look at an industry and figure out what was missing. I realized that no one was making fine, well-made hearts whiskey—or well-made moonshine, for that matter."

In and around Asheville, Troy & Sons is well on its way to becoming a tourist destination. They're not going to displace

State of the art: the still at Troy and Sons, manufactured by the German still maker Kothe. COURTESY TROY & SONS DISTILLERY

Moonshine Nation

Biltmore Estate as an attraction anytime soon, but the distillery is averaging around five thousand visitors annually (in fact, the night before, during a casual conversation with a taxi driver, he made a point of telling my wife and me that we had to go there). Unfortunately, the operation is hampered by the fact that they can't sell whiskey from their front door. North Carolina is a control state, which means that the sale of alcohol is restricted to state-run stores, a situation that Troy is lobbying to change.

One of the most effective aspects of her one-woman crusade has been her efforts to promote moonshine as a component of American cocktails, and one of her major accomplishments in that area has been penetrating Disney, a property that swore they would never sell moonshine. Troy & Sons was selected for their core list the first year and is currently featured in the best-selling cocktail at the Wilderness Lodge at Disney World. Later that day, at a restaurant in Asheville, we were able to try one of her creations: Sprig Fever, composed of Troy & Sons Platinum, muddled strawberries, rosemary simple syrup, club soda, and fresh lemon juice, lightly carbonated and delicious.

I wonder to what extent her two children determined the course of her business career—did that experience condition her to overcome obstacles?

"What it taught me was that I had to be a fighter. I was always focused, but when I had the boys I suddenly had to deal with a whole range of issues: keeping them alive, finding the right doctors, getting the schools to provide well for them. I became really tough and determined, and not afraid to go after something. In this business, you need all that and more. You have to have a lot of dedication and perseverance, along with the ability to see a problem and work around it to find a solution. If you sit back in this business," she laughs, "you're not going to win."

RECIPES
Courtesy of Troy & Sons

American Mule

1½ ounces Troy & Sons Platinum
1 ounce Domaine de Canton ginger liqueur
1 lemon wedge
Soda water

Pour Platinum and ginger liqueur over ice in short rocks glass. Squeeze and drop in lemon wedge; top with soda and mix well.

Carolina Sunset

1½ ounces Troy & Sons Platinum
½ ounce Aperol
½ ounce fresh lemon juice
1 dash simple syrup
2–3 ounces soda water
1 orange slice

Combine all ingredients except soda and orange slice and shake with ice. Strain into an ice-filled Collins glass and top with soda; garnish with orange slice.

Troyberry Lemonade

1½ ounces Troy & Sons Platinum
½ ounce raspberry liqueur
3 lemon wedges
Splash of soda water
Sugar for rimming glass (optional)

Pour Platinum and raspberry liqueur into a shaker and squeeze in lemon wedges; shake well and strain over ice into short rocks glass. Add splash of soda water (optional: rim glass with sugar before pouring).

Platinum Luau

1 ounce Troy & Sons Platinum
1 ounce Lillet Blonde
1 ounce pineapple juice
Soda water
3 lemon twists

Pour all ingredients over fresh ice in a tall rocks glass, top with soda water, and garnish with lemon twists.

Asheville Bramble

- **1½ ounces Troy & Sons Platinum**
- **¾ ounce fresh lemon juice**
- **¾ ounce simple syrup**
- **¾ ounce crème de mûre**
- **2 blackberries**

Pour all ingredients into a shaker with ice and shake vigorously. Strain into an ice-filled highball glass and garnish with blackberries.

White Hound Martini

- **2 ounces Troy & Sons Platinum**
- **1 ounce triple sec**
- **2½ ounces grapefruit juice**
- **Dash of grenadine**
- **1 lemon twist**

Pour Platinum, triple sec, grapefruit juice, and grenadine into a shaker with ice. Shake vigorously, strain into a chilled, tall rocks glass, and garnish with lemon twist.

Chilled Troytottie

1 lemon wedge
Dash of cinnamon sugar
2 dashes Angostura bitters
2 ounces Troy & Sons Platinum
3–4 ounces hard apple cider
1 lemon slice
Ground cinnamon

In a highball glass, muddle lemon wedge, cinnamon sugar, and bitters. Top with Platinum; add ice and fill with cider. Stir well to combine. Garnish with lemon slice and ground cinnamon.

Harvest Moon Margarita

2 ounces Troy & Sons Oak Reserve
1½ ounces fresh lime juice
½ ounce fresh orange juice
1½ ounces Monin agave nectar
1 lime wedge

Pour all ingredients into a shaker with ice. Shake vigorously and strain over ice into rocks glass. Garnish with lime wedge.

☆ ☆ ☆

HOWLING MOON

It's an understatement to say that Cody Bradford and Chivous Downey have moonshine in their blood: The DNA for corn whiskey has been firmly embedded in their chromosomes for generations; if not centuries. Cody's father, Darick; uncle Ernie; great-uncle; grandfather Theron; great-grandfather; and great-great-grandfather were all moonshiners. Both of Chivous's grandfathers, along with his step-grandfather, made corn liquor in the hills.

"Almost everybody you meet up here in the mountains of western North Carolina has some member of their family that was connected to it in some way," says Chivous. "People were very poor, and just about everybody made it to survive."

"Most folks around here grew corn," adds Cody. "It was supposed to be a cash crop, but they couldn't haul it to market—the only way for them to get it there was to distill it first. It was a barter economy. If they took the corn to the mill, they'd pay the miller in cornmeal for grinding it. Liquor was one of the few things you could actually get money for."

Their moonshine memories were forged at an early age. Chivous remembers taking his first gulp of corn liquor at six or seven. "I could never figure out what was going on with my grandparents. They had these jugs of water—or what I thought was water—all over the house, and stashed in the barn and chicken coop. Then one day, one of my little cousins was cutting his teeth, and my grandfather took some of the stuff from the jugs and rubbed it on his gums. He gave me a sip, and I spit it up," he laughs. "I was expecting water."

The two young men have been best friends since the eighth grade and went to high school together. After graduation Cody headed off to the University of North Carolina at Asheville to study history; Chivous entered the Marines and served in Afghanistan. Four years later, when Cody had his degree and Chivous's enlistment was up, they returned home to find a situation ironically similar to what their ancestors had been dealing with for generations: The economy was bad, and there were no jobs to be had.

"I graduated in 2007," says Cody, "and nobody was hiring around here. I really did like history, but I couldn't have done much with it unless I got a PhD. It was the same thing for Chivous—when he got out of the service, he couldn't find work. So we really got into this because there wasn't anything else to do."

"We had a succession of dead-end jobs," adds Chivous. "We spent about two years working for a company that managed nursing homes, and kicked around a lot after that. After a while we realized we'd be better off on our own, creating our own business."

Had they talked about doing moonshine previously, and were they attracted to the culture?

"When we were growing up, we never discussed moonshine," says Cody. "It was such as serious offense, it was just something you didn't talk about. Used to be that if you even had part of a still, you'd go to federal prison if they caught you.

"We had actually talked about doing it illegally, but it's just too hard now to go out into the woods and make it. Most of the

Generations of moonshiners: Darick, Uncle Ernie, and Cody (left to right).
COURTESY HOWLING MOON DISTILLERY

Moonshine Nation

land either belongs to the government, or there's someone living less than a mile away. My family was very supportive, but they didn't trust the government after all those years—they wanted us to make sure that our permits were in order. So after it was legalized, we jumped on it."

"They were probably forced to legalize it," adds Chivous. "The moonshine culture is so pervasive around here, they'd just continue to lose money if they didn't legalize it. And losing money, that's the one thing they hate."

And what about their parents—were they supportive, or did they want something more refined for their children than the moonshine culture in which they grew up?

"My dad helped us get going," laughs Cody. "He gave us the recipe and helped us fine-tune it. His only concern was that we wouldn't get in trouble. Nowadays they can track everything— that's one of the reasons moonshine died out. They can follow truckloads of sugar by helicopter if they want to."

"We sat out in the woods for a few years before we went legal," says Chivous. "We'd listen to the old-timers telling stories about how they did things—what recipes they used, how they ran their stills. Our families gave us advice, too, but it was a lot of trial and error."

Their operation, Howling Moon distillery, is located in a small building on the outskirts of Asheville. They run three small stills made for them by local fabricators—the same craftsmen who constructed Popcorn Sutton's stills, in fact. Their small plant is capable of turning out about four hundred gallons per week. At present their product is only available in North Carolina, but it has created a sensation.

Cody Bradford and Chivous Downey are committed to the idea of producing true mountain moonshine, the kind of whiskey that flourished in the Appalachian hills for centuries.

"It's a dying art," says Cody. "Before we started this, I tried a lot of the stuff on the market, and most of it wasn't really moonshine—it was just vodka, basically. So we wanted to get a real traditional moonshine out there, so that people would know what it's like."

"That's right," agrees Chivous. "We wanted people to know what their ancestors were drinking up in these mountains 150 years ago."

"Moonshine is a very specific product with a style all its own," says Cody. "You know it when you taste it. Because of the lack of standards, though, people can make vodka and call it moonshine. Then it reflects back on us—people drink our stuff and think it's too rough, because they're used to vodka."

At the time of my visit, Howling Moon distillery is really an oversize shed, with a main room that houses the three stills. With the exception of heat supplied by propane gas, those stills are a faithful replica of what you might have found up in the hills a century ago; one of them, in fact, is fitted with a condenser used by Cody's great-great-grandfather. Their moonshine is bottled at the traditional 100 proof, and it is remarkably good—redolent of corn on the nose, rich and forceful on the palate, with pepper accents set against a very smooth texture. At $24.95, it is priced well below competing products, many of which are inferior. There are two distinctive fruit infusions, Strawberry and Apple Pie, and a few other flavors in development.

"These are traditional moonshine stills," says Cody, "but definitely not your typical whiskey still. I know people who've been to Scotland and toured the scotch distilleries, and they say that the stills over there are a lot like these, except that they use stainless steel instead of copper.

Theron Edwards, grandfather of Howling Moon's Cody Bradford, with his still. COURTESY HOWLING MOON DISTILLERY

"Making something by hand is foreign to a lot of people nowadays. We come from the kind of background where we grow our own food, and raise hogs and chickens. Most people now, when they need something, they go to the store and buy it. When I was born, though, my father was a tobacco farmer and moonshiner. We canned our own food and made our own preserves."

As we taste, I spot a bottle of Tim Smith Moonshine on a corner table, and ask them what they think of the *Moonshiners* TV show.

"We're all friends," says Cody.

"Well," laughs Chivous, "it's TV, you know."

"But they're doing a great thing, really," says Cody. "I wouldn't say that all of it is 100 percent accurate, but they've created a lot of publicity for moonshine, and that's important."

I ask them why they think moonshine has captured the imagination of the public in such a compelling way.

"Part of it's the fascination with genealogy," says Chivous. "People have been doing a lot of research about their ancestry. Folks around here are curious about the role moonshine may have played in their family history."

"America has always been captivated by outlaws," explains Cody. "Look at Popcorn Sutton. People love that stuff. They love Jesse James and Billy the Kid. And Lewis Redmond—he was the most famous outlaw in America at one time."

Remember "Major" Lewis Redmond, the Robin Hood of the Dark Corner? For these guys, he's not a historical figure that lived more than a century ago: To them, Redmond is as real as a desperado who lives around the corner. And in a bizarre twist of history, the great-great-uncle of Cody's wife was Alfred Duckworth, the federal agent killed by Lewis Redmond at the very beginning of his career as an outlaw.

"Redmond got sick of running from the law," says Cody, "so he told them he was going to kill all of them. The revenuers got so scared that half of them locked themselves in the Pickens County jail to avoid him. They finally decided to leave town and stop pursuing him. Redmond killed a lot of people, but he didn't get credit for most of them. It was so secluded up here that no one really knew what was going on. They kidnapped his friend Amos Ladd at one point, and Redmond personally ambushed the posse transporting Ladd and shot and killed about half of them. There was another instance where a guy had informed on some moonshiners to the revenuers. Redmond walked right up to him in a field and shot him dead. You don't hear about a lot of that stuff. Many times he'd be pursued by people trying to capture him, and he'd take a knife and gut them—up one side and down the other, so that their guts just fell out. He was one of the meanest men who ever lived, I would say. But at the same time, he was a good guy who did a lot for people around here."

"That's right," agrees Chivous. "That's absolutely right."

"He just did what he had to do," says Cody. "Everybody was scared to death of him. When they finally caught him, they put about six bullets in him and left him in a field to die. They were too scared to even check if he was still alive, which he was. The *New York Times* actually printed his obituary."

Cody shows me a picture of his grandfather.

"He grew up around here, mostly in Burnsville like I did. His father died in 1925 when he was two years old, and he started working at eight. He would hire himself out with a team of oxen and plow for people. Other than that, moonshine was the only way he had to make money. Him and his brother made liquor up here for years and years.

"We talk about this being the frontier. One of my ancestors back around 1810, his name was Howard Higgins. He was a blacksmith and had come over from Ireland. I did some research into my genealogy and found a letter he wrote when he was a kid. He talks about sitting on the edge of the farm in Burnsville and guarding for Indians. This whole area was Cherokee territory, and there were a lot of Indian attacks. Back then, this was about as far West as you could get."

I mention my theory that the Whiskey Rebellion, with its imposition of taxes on farmers and small distillers, was the source of most of today's divisions in society, and he agrees.

"If you study it," he says, "you see that even back in Scotland it was a tax issue—that's why my ancestors got run out of Scotland. The Scots sent them to Northern Ireland to settle. Then the English started raising the price of rents and everything else there, so they left and came to America. And after they fight the Revolution to get free of taxes here from England, the first thing that happens is they get hit with taxes again.

"I can trace my family back to the 1700s in this area. They were a tough group, because they were used to fighting constantly through the generations. And after the Whiskey Rebellion they moved out here to Indian territory—you don't think of North Carolina that way, but it was. They moved into the middle of hostile land, and they fought tooth and nail to keep it. Most of them were making whiskey when they got here, or they married into families that did. Almost every branch of my family has some moonshine background. I had some relatives during Prohibition who said they had found a silver mine back in the hills," he laughs, "and they always had money. Of course they were making moonshine back there, but to this day I have some relatives who are still looking for that silver mine."

The history student is in full stride now, and you can't help thinking that he would have made as good a professor as he is a moonshiner.

"These were the same people who fought the Battle of King's Mountain. They were told by Patrick Ferguson, who was the commander of the English militia, that his forces would be coming through this area. This region was originally known as the State of Franklin, or the Free Republic of Franklin—they had tried to break off from the English even before the Revolution, so they were an independent group to start with. The goal of the army as they passed through an area was to pick up recruits, and the British needed them desperately. Ferguson sent a letter to John Sevier, who was the head of the Continental militia, telling him that if the locals tried to interfere with the British Army, they would burn their houses down. So the residents marched from Tennessee and North Carolina to King's Mountain, which was in

South Carolina at that time. They fought Ferguson and defeated him. It was one of the turning points of the Revolution, because it sent Cornwallis into retreat."

In fact, it was a rout. The Battle of King's Mountain took place on October 7, 1780, with the colonists taking the British Army by surprise. Ferguson was shot and killed during the battle, which forced Lord Cornwallis to abandon his planned invasion of North Carolina. Cody's account of the proceedings is just as vivid and detailed as a football fan's recollection of the game on Monday

Darick Bradford, Cody's father, in the field where he grows the corn for Howling Moon. COURTESY HOWLING MOON DISTILLERY

morning. This type of reverence for military history is not unusual in the South, of course, but generally the topic of discussion is the Civil War rather than the Revolution.

I ask him if the revenuers in this part of the state were honest, or if they took bribes.

"Sure," he laughs, "they all did. They were crooked as hell. Everybody hated them, and there was a lot of them that got killed around here too. My father-in-law used to be a sheriff, and he could tell you all kinds of stories. If you look back to Lewis Redmond's time, half the agents they got were outlaws themselves. They figured it took a crook to catch a crook. But the problem is, if you give a crook a badge, then he's just a crook with a badge. My father-in-law is a good example. He was a moonshiner himself, so he knew where they were and how to chase them. But he was crooked too—most of them were.

"If you look at movies like *Lawless*, you'll see what went on. That's a true story. It takes place in Franklin County, Tennessee, during Prohibition, where all the local guys were bought off. Then the feds came in and demanded a bigger cut, and the moonshiners refused. It was all-out war. The main federal guy involved in that actually got indicted after Prohibition.

"My great-uncle was arrested one time, and when he went to court, the judge turned out to be somebody who bought liquor off him. And the DA was a customer of his, too. They couldn't just let him go, so they gave him the smallest possible fine. Most of the time, they didn't want to arrest the guys who made the good liquor. They always tried to bust the ones who made the stuff that would kill you.

"In a lot of ways, Prohibition was the worst thing that happened to moonshine. A lot of people got into it who didn't know what they were doing, and they made rotgut whiskey. People were using car radiators, making stuff that had antifreeze in it, and it gave moonshine a bad name. Folks like my family didn't want to be associated with that—their moonshine legacy went way back, to the time when it was both a craft and an art.

"Anyway, this kind of stuff has always gone on. If you look back to Lewis Redmond's time, you'll see that there was a lot of payoffs. The governor of South Carolina actually sent the posse in the wrong direction, then sat down and had dinner with Redmond. But everything escalated after the Civil War, when they revived the whiskey tax—it really took off, and it hasn't stopped since."

Slowly and gradually, the two men are discovering the boom in mixology that seems to be driving many of today's liquor trends. Although their preference is still drinking moonshine straight from the jar (Chivous's favorite is "moonshine on the rocks, hold the rocks"), they've come to realize that, for many of us, bartenders are the driving force in the world of spirits. Howling Moon has begun to be featured in designer cocktails served at some of downtown Asheville's hottest restaurants. "When I first got into this," says Chivous, "I wasn't real familiar with the whole cocktail scene and how it has evolved. But I've been really impressed with the creativity that a lot of these bartenders and bar managers show when they come up with some of these cocktails."

As we sit there chatting, Cody and Chivous discuss plans to expand Howling Moon. Up to that point they had been approached by distributors in a number of states, but hadn't been able to produce enough liquor to supply the pipeline; they also had offers from outside investors, but wanted to keep control of the operation themselves. They eventually ordered a 750-gallon still and expanded their mashing area, which increased their capacity by 60 percent. Their eventual goal is to move into a larger building, which would allow them to distribute their moonshine beyond North Carolina, and to remain self-financed.

Their goal is "slow, natural, and organic growth," but even that might prove to be a challenge. When you look at the exploding craft distilling category in America, you see many similar outfits that are making the transition from small and casual garage operations to large national brands. While some have changed for the worse, there are also cases of distillers who have maintained the quality of their product as they experienced dramatic growth— Patrón tequila is a good example, and there are others. At the very least, the nature of your business changes. You become much more concerned with balance sheets and far more involved in managing the product flow to different markets around the country. You hire more employees and face the challenge of finding people who feel the same way about your mission as you do. You spend more and more time traveling, riding around strange cities in cars with distributor salespeople as you call on wholesale customers and tell your story. The future of Howling Moon will be interesting to follow, and my guess is that Cody Bradford and Chivous Downey will maintain the legacy of their ancestors that propelled them to this point.

RECIPES
Courtesy of Howling Moon

Tea to the Moon

1 tea bag
8 ounces hot water
2 ounces Howling Moon moonshine (White or Apple Pie)
¼ lemon
Honey

Steep tea bag in hot water. Add moonshine, lemon juice, and honey to taste. Serve either hot or chilled.

Howling Bloody Moon

1½ ounces Howling Moon moonshine
8 ounces Bloody Mary mix
Pickled okra
Green olives
Lemon and lime wedges

Mix moonshine and Bloody Mary mix together in a highball glass with ice and stir; garnish with okra, olives, and citrus.

Howling Moonjito

6 mint leaves
4 parts fresh lime juice
2 parts simple syrup
3 parts Howling Moon moonshine
Soda water
Lime wedge

Muddle mint leaves together with lime juice and simple syrup at bottom of a highball glass; add ice and moonshine; top with splash of soda water and garnish with lime wedge.

Strawberry Moonrita

1½ ounces Howling Moon Strawberry
½ ounce triple sec
½ ounce strawberry puree
3 ounces sour mix
Splash of orange juice
Strawberry, lime slice, or orange slice, for garnish

Combine ingredients in a shaker with ice and shake vigorously; strain into a chilled cocktail glass, or serve over ice in a highball glass. Garnish with strawberry, lime slice, or orange slice.

Mountain Moonrita

Salt, for rimming glass (optional)
2 ounces Howling Moon moonshine
8 ounces orange juice
8 ounces sour mix
Splash of Grand Marnier
Lime wedge

Rim glass with salt, if desired. Combine ingredients in a shaker with ice and shake vigorously. Strain into a margarita glass and garnish with fresh lime wedge.

POPCORN SUTTON: FICTION AND FACT

We live in a world dominated by celebrities. While this may be annoying (to some of us, hopefully, at certain moments), there's no doubt that famous people are creating a number of modern trends. In many cases they are paid to do so, and with good reason: There are millions of Americans with their noses pressed against the glass, staring in wonder at their idols who seem to be living such rich and rewarding lives.

In the popular imagination, one of the drivers of the moonshine trend has been Marvin "Popcorn" Sutton. For starters, he was the ultimate moonshiner from central casting—a foul-mouthed, homespun guy with a scraggly white beard, perpetually clad in overalls, full of quaint expressions and backwoods wisdom. He became a living icon, a symbol of moonshine culture for many of us, and his popularity and notoriety only increased after his death.

Prior to developing an interest in moonshine, I had not heard of Popcorn Sutton; had I closed my eyes and pictured a moonshiner, however, I would have conjured up an image of someone very similar to him.

Popcorn was dead by the time I started doing research for this book, and a line of legal moonshine had been launched in his name: Popcorn Sutton's Tennessee White Whiskey. Alive or dead, I thought he would make an interesting subject for a profile. At one point I had a trip planned to Nashville, where the distillery was located, and I began the process of setting up an appointment to tour the facility and interview Jamey Grosser. Grosser had supposedly worked with Popcorn before his death, and was now the master distiller for the legal moonshine.

And then a curious thing happened. I went on the website, found an e-mail address, and sent a request for an appointment—three or four requests, actually, all of which went unanswered. There was no phone number listed on the website, so I surfed the web in search of an address and contact number. I found neither. At this point I did an extensive Internet search for two or three hours, taking a number of different approaches, and came up empty on all of them. The web seemed to be wiped clean of any mention of the distillery, not an easy thing to accomplish in the digital era. Nor was there any information on Jamey Grosser. I read every story that had been written about Grosser and Popcorn Sutton's Tennessee White Whiskey, contacted the people who wrote those stories in search of leads, and once again found none. I heard a rumor that the moonshine was being made on a contract basis at the Corsair Artisan Distillery in Nashville. At the time I was e-mailing back and forth with one of the principals at Corsair, since I planned on visiting them when I arrived in the city. After I asked this person whether his company was making the moonshine, he stopped communicating with me. Obviously a distillery had to exist, since the whiskey was being made somewhere, but you would have had a better chance of finding a missile silo in Russia than unearthing its location.

At this point you didn't have to be an investigative reporter to be intrigued by the situation. People turn down free publicity all the time, for any number of reasons, but businesses usually don't. The lack of Internet references was particularly baffling, since even a listing of the distillery's location would have resulted in dozens or hundreds of accidental backlinks. I was determined to find out more about Popcorn Sutton. Fortunately there was a good deal in the public record—books written about him and by him, along with some very powerful videos made toward the end of his career. I was able to track down three of his children, and had an extended conversation with one of them. Some of what I discovered broke the stereotype of his image, and a good deal of it was disturbing. I'll share as much as I can with you, because his story is a compelling example of American mythmaking.

Here are the facts:

Marvin "Popcorn" Sutton was born in North Carolina on October 5, 1946, and ended up in Cocke County, Tennessee. His father and grandfather were moonshiners. He began drinking liquor at the age of six, and by age twelve he was learning how to make wine. Shortly afterward he was apprenticed to his father in the moonshine trade. According to legend, he acquired his nickname by destroying a bar's popcorn vending machine with a pool cue.

For the last twenty years before his father's death, the two men made moonshine on Snowbird Mountain in Cocke County. Snowbird was extremely remote at the time, and remains difficult to find to this day. During those twenty years they were never caught—partly because they were careful, and partly because the dense forest of the mountain gave them a number of perfect hiding places. Popcorn later said they could have thrown a rock at a car on one of the nearby roads, and the driver would still have been unable to find them.

The Suttons were a self-contained operation: They made the moonshine and also sold it, primarily to wholesalers who resold it again. This practice limited their profit margin, but they were usually able to double their money and also avoid exposure to casual consumers who might turn them in. Their whiskey had the reputation of being the best in the area, with absolutely no heads or tails mixed in to stretch the run. "I never sold a man or woman a jar of likker that they didn't come back for some more," Popcorn said.

His problems with the law began after his father's death, during the publicity-seeking phase of his career. He was busted for the first time in August 1974 in Hartford, Tennessee, fined, and placed on probation. Popcorn had a new still made, took it back to the place where he had been arrested, and continued to make moonshine throughout his probation. "They [the authorities] wasn't hardly as smart as they thought they was," he said. "They don't think the same way I do. I took my new pot back to the same place where I'd been caught—back to the same furnace that they'd just pulled the pot out of . . . See, most people caught at a still site, you couldn't run them back there with a big stick. Me, I just went right back to the same furnace."

By anyone's standards, Popcorn was a brilliant marketer. Over a period of decades, he carefully constructed the image of the moonshiner that we have today: independent, irascible, defiant against the system. One of the grave markers he designed before his death read "Popcorn Said Fuck You," and that was his public stance—the guy who was constantly giving society the middle finger. In the beginning he appeared at county fairs throughout the South, dispensing sips of moonshine along with amusing stories and bits of distilling lore. In 1999 he wrote *Me and My Likker* with the help of one of his daughters, an autobiographical volume that gives a detailed description of how to make moonshine (just the kind of thing the authorities would appreciate, no doubt).

As the Internet age took hold and information became easier to access, his fame grew. He began giving interviews and making home videos. He appeared in *Mountain Talk*, a documentary by Neal Hutcheson, in 2002. Later that year he was the subject of a film called *This Is the Last Damn Run of Likker I'll Ever Make;* it was adapted into a 2008 documentary that won a Southeast Emmy Award and firmly established him in the public imagination. He also appeared in a number of other videos and films and was featured on the History Channel.

By now you probably perceive the fatal catch in Popcorn's marketing strategy. Photogenic and charismatic though he might have been, he was still doing something highly illegal. It's one thing to thumb your nose at the law and outrun them on the back roads of Appalachia, and quite another to humiliate the federal revenue bureaucracy in front of an audience of millions. As he garnered more publicity, he also drew increasing amounts of heat. His residence was raided on January 24, 1998, and federal agents seized sixty-two gallons of liquor worth $2,600; they had an automatic search warrant for the next year, but failed to find any more moonshine when they returned.

At numerous points over the next decade, Popcorn publicly declared that he was finished with moonshine. Since illicit distilling was the only skill he had and the only way for him to make a living, this claim didn't get him much credibility with the revenuers (he did launch a second career as a still manufacturer, a venture that was just as bad in the eyes of the law as moonshining). In January 2009 he was raided again by the ATF and sentenced to eighteen months in federal prison for selling illegal spirits and possession of a firearm as a felon. In a final act of defiance, he committed suicide by carbon monoxide poisoning on March 16, 2009, three days before he was supposed to report to prison.

After Popcorn's death, Hank Williams Jr. approached his widow, Pam, with the idea of producing a legal line of moonshine bearing the Popcorn Sutton name. The brand was launched in November 2010.

☆　☆　☆

What was it about Popcorn Sutton that made such a deep imprint on the American imagination?

There are various theories that make sense. Junior Johnson, who knew Popcorn over a period of decades, put it succinctly: "He was a crazy feller, and people like that." There's some truth to this—after sexy, people love crazy most of all. Cody Bradford's version contained a kernel of truth as well: "America has always been captivated by outlaws." If you doubt this, just look at the staggering number of books, TV shows, and movies devoted to glorifying the lifestyle of the mob.

My own theory is that when Popcorn extended his middle finger to society, he was tapping into a powerful and widespread current fantasy. Most people lead boring lives. Many live in gated communities with no character or soul; some are married to people they can't stand; even more are working for bosses they hate, doing jobs they can't figure out why they wanted in the first place. They secretly yearn to emulate Popcorn Sutton and say "fuck you" to everyone in their lives, at least for a while. He awakened the most profound desire of all: to have the courage to be yourself, to take control of your own life regardless of the cost.

Some of this comes through when you read *Me and My Likker*. The book paints a portrait of a man who was independent, quirky, and unconventional, and describes a side of Popcorn that many people might not have perceived. It is really worth reading because it paints an accurate portrait of what it was like to make mountain moonshine before it was legalized. Every phase of the operation— from still construction, selecting the corn (he insisted on using nonhybrid white corn), mashing, and distilling—was conducted with the utmost care, along with an uncompromising commitment to quality. Popcorn was very good at what he did, and extremely proud of his product and reputation. He gives unstinting credit to the people who mentored him and taught him the craft. He also goes to great lengths to dispel the image of moonshiners as lazy hillbillies, and at numerous points stresses that "making likker is the hardest work you have ever done."

However, that was only one aspect of the man, and his carefully constructed public image was another. Let's take a look at how that image was put together.

The best-known book on Popcorn probably isn't *Me and My Likker*. More likely it's *Popcorn Sutton: The Making and Marketing of a Hillbilly Hero*, with text by Tom Wilson Jester and photographs by Don Dudenbostel. The two men spent quite a bit of time with Popcorn in Cocke County and basically swallowed the legend whole, although they were aware he was using it for his own ends and made an effort to recover their balance toward the end of the book ("Hell, why not make money off this shit?" Popcorn told them, referring to his stories and pictures. "I do."). The photographs, which are striking, are easily the best part—the camera loved Popcorn.

To get the private side of the story, I made an effort to track down his children. This wasn't easy, since there were as many as seventeen of them by the same number of women; some of them may not have been aware of their heritage, and most weren't looking for publicity. The most revealing conversation I had was with Regina Sutton Chennault, who is now a respected trauma surgeon in Alaska. Her mother was Popcorn's first wife, and she was about twelve when they divorced. Dr. Chennault was both helpful and extremely generous with her time. Much of what she told me was disturbing, and some of it was chilling.

I began by asking her if she had been aware of her father's profession when she was growing up.

"Oh yes," she said. "My mother delivered liquor with me in the front seat. I grew up being a slave to the liquor business. I was constantly told to wash the jars, because we were going to make sauerkraut. Well, we never made sauerkraut. My mother always had me shelling corn—at first, I could never figure out what we were doing with all that corn."

I asked her if there had been any stigma attached to moonshine in her community.

"Many people describe my father in positive terms, but I'll tell you the flat-out truth about him. He was actually very smart, even though he dropped out of school early—he could play just about any musical instrument if he wasn't intoxicated or on drugs. When he was married to my mother, he was either high or drunk all the time. If I saw him almost beat my mother to death once, I saw it nearly a thousand times. He would do things that I found despicable, such as taking money out of collection jars that was earmarked for people who were terminally ill or who had had serious accidents.

"He was an extremely violent person. One of the most amazing things I saw when I was a small child occurred in Maggie Valley, where my grandparents lived. There was a barn where they used to make liquor. The men would all be standing out there at nighttime, and every weekend was a moonshine party. Anyway, one day there was a man beating at the back door of my Grandma Bonnie's kitchen. I was about four years old at the time, and I was in the living room with her and some other ladies. My grandma opened the door, and there was a man standing there with arterial blood pumping out of his neck. My father had stabbed this man with a butcher knife—like the biggest butcher knife you might find in your kitchen, and it was up to the handle in the guy's neck. It was actually one of the turning points in my life. I was always curious about the human body after that."

Ironically, the incident may have spurred her interest in a medical career.

"Anyway, after all this random violence and domestic violence, I'd hear people call him a hero. I don't see that at all. I view him as similar to a tornado that goes through a trailer park. He left a path of destruction behind him that was unbelievable. I always think of something that President Obama said, that he was shaped more by his father's absence than his presence. That was definitely true for me, since he was in prison so much of the time. When he wasn't, he'd go off and get drunk and not come back for days or weeks.

"Yes, it shaped me, but I knew from very early on that God and education would improve my life and keep me from being like him."

I asked if she had a relationship with her siblings growing up, or if that came later.

"It came much later on. I always thought I was an only child, to be honest. I found out about Sky after my father died—I hadn't been aware of her, although she apparently knew of my existence (she was referring to Sky Sutton, author of *Daddy Moonshine*). My father married her mother and carried on with the same pattern: drugs, drinking, leaving her alone up in the hills with a newborn baby. I had never spent much time on the Internet, but one day I sat down at the computer and typed 'Marvin Sutton' into Google. And when I typed in his name, Sky's name came up as well, along with her book. So I sent her an e-mail and told her that Marvin Sutton had been my father. And she answered back immediately, saying that I was her half-sister and that she had been looking for me her entire life. As I talked to her, I found out about some of the other half-siblings."

Was the hillbilly image constructed for the public, or was it real?

"Well, he *was* a hillbilly—I doubt that he ever had on a suit and tie in his life. He always wore the overalls, with the long-sleeved checkered shirt underneath. They all dressed like that. My father could have done just about anything he wanted to; he was extremely bright, and obviously he was a chemist. When you ask about the image, you're probably referring to the book by Jester and Dudenbostel. They floated the idea that my father had put the image out there to get publicity, but he was really like that. He was a lot like those guys in the movie *Lawless*. He would just go out with a bunch of liquor and drugs and women, and stay out as long as he could."

What about Popcorn Sutton's Tennessee White Whiskey?

"I think that's unfortunate, because it's not what his moonshine tasted like. I have the recipe he actually used, which came from my grandfather, and it's locked up in a bank vault. It's the biggest joke

I've ever heard, because when I visited his widow Pam back in 2009, she was asking me how to make moonshine. And now she has this business with some guy who supposedly worked with him for a few days."

"You mean Jamey Grosser?"

"Yes."

"I heard Corsair was actually making the moonshine for them."

"That's true. But it's not Sutton moonshine—it doesn't taste the same, and it's not made the same way. They're just mass-producing it and gluing their label on it. Jamey Grosser told me that he owns my father's name and image, which I think is strange."

I asked about the controversy surrounding Popcorn's burial.

"My Dad made wills constantly, depending on his situation at the time. But he gave his last will to a bunch of different people. He was very clear that he wanted to be buried near my grandparents, in what you might call the family cemetery, and that's where he was buried initially. Then Pam told me she was going to move my father. I asked why, and she showed me a copy of a 'corrected' will that had a lot of things scratched out and changed, and the changes were supposedly initialed by my father. She believed that will gave her the power to do that. She told me that she was going to turn the house into a museum about my father—he's buried in the front yard right now, which I think is odd. Obviously I'd like to see him back with my grandparents, but there isn't anything I can do about it."

Why does she think that moonshiners have become folk heroes, much in the same way as mobsters?

"I don't disagree that they're folk heroes to a lot of people. I'm not negative about Appalachian moonshiners in general, because some of them did very positive things. Many of them were hardworking, intelligent people who made liquor, but they used the money to support their families and help the community. But in the case of my father, I know there wasn't one good or positive thing about the man. I'm proud of my heritage, but not of him. I'm not saying that he never helped anyone—maybe he did, but he never helped his wives or children.

"I'll tell you one more story about one of my half-sisters. This one came along later, but it was the same pattern, living with him up in the woods. Men would come over to the house to buy moonshine from him, and he would offer her up to have sex with them, after which they paid him. It put her on a bad course, and she recently died of drugs and alcohol."

I also communicated with Sky Sutton and read her book *Daddy Moonshine.* Sky's mother left Popcorn when she was a toddler, and she has no childhood memories of him. Nor did she have any contact with him afterward—she did call and talk to him two or three times as an adult, but it never resulted in a father-daughter relationship. "Marvin Sutton and I have never been formally introduced," she says in the book.

"In some cases," comments Popcorn in *Me and My Likker,* "I have a heart as big as Texas and in some cases it is not as big as a God-damn gnat's ass." Sky's comment on this is: "I guess I got the gnat's ass end of my father's heart."

Daddy Moonshine is an interesting book on many levels. Even though she grew up in New England, she has a deep respect for the culture of Cocke County, where she was born. "The endangered craft of moonshining and the ways of mountain people are a disappearing part of American history," she writes. "I'm proud of my heritage. I want to be one of the voices that keep the old ways known."

She is definitely one of those voices. Her book quotes liberally from *Me and My Likker* and presents an accurate picture of the moonshine process. Her view of Popcorn, however, is considerably more complicated. "He may be a phenomenal moonshiner," she says, "but, sadly, he's a complete loss as a father." On the other hand, she feels that Popcorn's life "gives us a portrait of a culture that is quickly being deleted by big box stores, McMansions, and fully paved highways." Ironically, her book was finished just as Popcorn was committing suicide, and this even seems to have shaken her profoundly—perhaps because it was the final chapter in a saga of emotional loss.

When I finished *Daddy Moonshine*, I was sufficiently confused by her ambivalent attitude toward him that I e-mailed her again. Did she have the luxury of a positive view of her father, I wondered, because she didn't know him personally?

She assured me that there were thousands of hours of anguish behind any positive words she might have written. She also said that her private feelings were just that—private—and would remain so, which I respected. As to her ambivalence: "My father was a brilliant man in his own way," she wrote. "There's no getting around that. He was larger than life before he died and even more so since he's passed. These things must be recognized and respected. If the story is to remain accurate harsh judgment is to be avoided."

☆ ☆ ☆

Call it karma if you like, but Popcorn Sutton's Tennessee White Whiskey has had a rocky time since its launch in 2010.

The current controversy surrounding the product is a trademark infringement lawsuit brought against the company by Jack Daniel's. When the Popcorn Sutton moonshine first hit the market, it was sold in the traditional mason jars. Sometime in 2012 they switched to a square bottle similar to the one that holds Jack Daniel's. On top of that, the black label features white lettering in a font that resembles the iconic Jack Daniel's design.

The position of Jack Daniel's is that the Popcorn Sutton bottle and label design are intended to "deceive and confuse the public" into believing that there is some connection between the two products, and that the Popcorn Sutton moonshine might be "a new Tennessee white whiskey in the Jack Daniel's line." The case was filed in US District Court in Nashville and was pending at press time; as of this writing, Popcorn Sutton Tennessee White Whiskey was available only in Kentucky, Tennessee, Georgia, and Texas.

Based on historical evidence, it's fairly easy to imagine Popcorn's reaction to all this if he were still with us. "Fuck Jack Daniel's," he'd probably say, grinning broadly and extending his middle finger. "Who needs their fucking square bottle anyway?"

☆ ☆ ☆

AMERICAN MOONSHINE PRODUCERS

The US government currently has no legal definition of moonshine. Virtually every other spirit approved for sale in America has to conform to the Federal Standards of Identity formulated by the TTB (Alcohol and Tobacco Tax and Trade Bureau, the successor to the BATF, or Bureau of Alcohol, Tobacco, and Firearms). Thus, while we have very specific regulations about bourbon, rye, brandy, vodka, or gin, moonshine remains a mystery.

This raises the time-honored question: If it's legal, can it really be moonshine? In some cases the products currently being marketed and sold as moonshine are faithful replicas of the liquor once made in makeshift stills up in the Appalachian hills; in other instances the spirit in the bottle is little more than vodka. Most people would probably say that moonshine is unaged whiskey made from a mash bill of sugar and corn, but other ingredients are often used as well.

To be listed in this chapter, a distiller had to make liquor that they called moonshine. Spirits labeled as corn whiskey, white whiskey, or white dog were excluded, even though some of those are very fine products. The fact that they are listed here is not a representation of their authenticity, although many of these distillers had family connections to the moonshine heritage. One further caveat: This is not a complete list. Moonshine is a hot category at the moment, and craft distilleries are sprouting up like mushrooms in a damp forest. At the time this list was compiled, there were at least twelve to fifteen moonshines in development, and by the time it appears in print there may be even more.

Compiling this list was made more difficult by the fact that many moonshine producers—particularly the smaller ones— seem determined to wrap themselves in an impenetrable cloak of secrecy, as if their product was still illegal. In a number of cases, prolonged digging was necessary to even verify the identity of some distilleries and products, so one can only imagine the difficulty consumers might have in attempting to buy them.

Alabama

High Ridge Spirits

Bullock County Rd. 7, Stills Crossroads, AL 36081;
(334) 738-2523

highridgespirits.com; info@highridgespirits.com

High Ridge was Alabama's first legal distillery since Prohibition was established there in 1915 (yes, they got a head start on the rest of the country). They produce 100-proof Stills Crossroads Alabama 'Shine, currently distributed within the state.

Visits: Unknown.

Arkansas

Arkansas Moonshine (formerly Uncle Ed's Moonshine)

PO Box 733, Melbourne, AR 72556; (870) 373-0888

arkansasmoonshine.com; info@arkansasmoonshine.com

A small craft distiller producing Arkansas Blue Flame Moonshine, corn whiskey bottled at 80 proof. Currently distributed only within the state.

Visits: No public tours, but private visits can be arranged.

Rock Town Distillery

1216 E. 6th St., Little Rock AR 72202; (501) 907-5244
arkansaslightning.com; info@rocktowndistillery.com
First legal distillery in the state since Prohibition; produces
Arkansas Lightning, a clear corn whiskey in two sizes (375 and
750 milliliters) and two proof levels (125 and 100, respectively),
along with fruit infusions (Apple Pie, Blueberry Cobbler, Grape,
and Peach). Currently distributed in nine states.

Visits: Tours offered seven days per week (twice daily, three on
Saturday); $7 admission includes tasting for visitors over twenty-
one.

CALIFORNIA

Ascendant Spirits

37 Industrial Way, Ste. 103, Buellton, CA 93427; (805) 691-1000
ascendantspirits.com; info@ascendantspirits.com
Ascendant is the first craft distillery in Santa Barbara, a region
better known for wine. It was opened in 2011 by Stephen
Gertman, and produces Silver Lightning Moonshine (99 proof),
made from 100 percent sweet yellow corn. Currently distributed
in California only.

Visits: Open for tastings and tours on Friday from 4 to 8 p.m.
and Saturday and Sunday from 1 to 7 p.m.

Fog's End Distillery

425 Alta St., Bldg. 15, Gonzalez, CA 93926; (831) 809-5941
fogsenddistillery.com; fogsenddistillery.craig@gmail.com
A small artisan distillery owned and operated by Craig Pakish,
making California Moonshine (100 proof) and White Dog (80
proof). Distributed in California and Illinois.
Visits: By appointment.

Tahoe Mountain Distillery

1611 Shop St. #4B, South Lake Tahoe, CA 96150;
(530) 416-0313
tahoemoonshine.net; tahoemoonshine@sbcglobal.net
Jeff Van Hee is making five different spirits at this micro-
distillery—among them 80-proof Tahoe Moonshine Stormin'
Whiskey, made from non-GMO corn and aged in used
Canadian whiskey barrels. Available in California and Nevada.
Visits: Unknown.

Valley Spirits

3085 Farrar Ave., Ste. #1, Modesto, CA 95354
drinkvalleyspirits.com
No phone or e-mail given

Valley Spirits is the brainchild of Lee Palleschi, who grew up watching his father make wine in the basement and eventually went on a quest to learn the distilling trade. He makes Outlaw Moonshine (99 proof), unaged and distilled from California wheat. It's unclear whether the product has any connection to the Moonshine Bandits, a biker band.

Visits: Unknown.

COLORADO

Mystic Mountain Distillery

11505 Spring Valley Rd., Larkspur, CO 80118; (303) 663-9375
mysticmtnspirits.com; info@mysticmtnspirits.com

Producers of Rocky Mountain Moonshine Sippin' Hooch, a corn whiskey available in 80- and 101-proof versions; extensive distribution in Colorado only.

Visits: Unknown.

Two Guns Distillery

401 Harrison Ave., Leadville, CO 80461; (970) 433-4527
twogunsdistillery.com; tgdistillery@gmail.com

B. A. Dallas, professional artist turned distiller, makes the Single Six Rocky Mountain Moonshine (100 proof) at ten thousand feet; limited distribution in Colorado only.

Visits: Tours and tastings offered daily, and walk-ins welcome; call to confirm specific times.

CONNECTICUT

Onyx Moonshine

64-D Oakland Ave., Hartford, CT 06108; (860) 550-1939
onyxmoonshine.com

Founded in 2011, Onyx became New England's first legal moonshine since Prohibition. Onyx Moonshine is available in 80- and 111-proof versions, and has limited in-state distribution.

Visits: Tours by appointment.

Florida

Flagler Spirits

23 Hargrove Grade, Ste. B, Palm Coast, FL 32137;
(386) 986-0641
flaglerspirits.com

James Day established Flagler Spirits in 2010. Among his products is Flagler Lightning, an 80-proof corn-based moonshine. Distribution is local.

Visits: Unknown.

GEORGIA

Free Spirits Distillery

415 Hwy. 53 E, Dawsonville, GA 30534; (770) 401-1211; (706) 344-1210

dawsonvillemoonshinedistillery.com; moonshiners@ dawsonvillemoonshinedistillery.com

Free Spirits makes Dawsonville Moonshine, based in one of the many places claiming to be the "moonshine capital of the world." The company was named for Simmie Free, a famous Appalachian moonshiner, and is apparently owned by his granddaughter; the distiller is Dwight "Punch" Bearden, a fourth-generation practitioner. Dawsonville Moonshine is an 86-proof corn whiskey actually made in the same building that houses the City Hall and the Georgia Racing Hall of Fame— nice work if you can get it.

Visits: Tours available daily.

Georgia Distilling Company

121 Blandy Way, Milledgeville, GA 31061; (478) 453-1086

georgiadistilling.com

This company manufactures Bear Creek Sippin' Shine, as well as a corn whiskey called Grandaddy Mimm's, but no information was available on either product.

Visits: No tours currently available.

Illinois

Mastermind Vodka

4262 State Hwy 62, Pontoon Beach, IL 62040; (855) 668-6352
mastermindvodka.com; tours@mastermindvodka.com
This vodka producer is now making LPR Moonshine, available at the distillery and through the Internet.

Visits: Tours available, if you want to watch them make vodka.

Iowa

Iowa Distilling Company

4349 Cumming Ave., Cumming, IA 50061; (515) 981-4216
iowadistilling.com
Iowa Distilling is committed to bringing the distillation process back to its farm roots. Among other products, they make Iowa Shine, an 80-proof corn whiskey made from corn purchased from a local farmer's co-op and ground on the premises. Distribution in Iowa only.

Visits: Tours and tastings offered on Tuesday from 4 to 8 p.m. and Saturday from noon to 5 p.m., or by appointment.

Kentucky

Barrel House Distilling Co.

**1200 Manchester St., Bldg. 9, Lexington, KY 40504;
(859) 259-0159**

barrelhousedistillery.com; barrelhousedistillery@yahoo.com

Barrel House was founded by two friends, Jeff Wiseman and Peter Wright, after inspiration struck them during a poker game. Among their spirits is 90-proof Devil John Moonshine, named for a Kentucky Civil War soldier, lawman, and moonshiner. Available in most states.

Visits: Tasting room open Wednesday through Friday from noon to 5 p.m. and Saturday and Sunday from 11 a.m. to 3 p.m.; tours available during those times.

Limestone Branch Distillery

**1280 Veterans Memorial Pkwy., Lebanon, KY 40033;
(270) 699-9004**

limestonebranch.com; info@limestonebranch.com

Limestone Branch is owned and operated by Steve and Paul Beam, members of Kentucky's most illustrious distilling family; their facility is located about seven miles from Maker's Mark. Their spirits include T.J. Pottinger Sugar Shine, a 100-proof corn whiskey, and various fruit infusions (Apple Cinnamon Pie, Pumpkin Pie, and Strawberry).

Visits: Tours given Monday through Saturday from 10 a.m to 5 p.m., Sunday from 1 to 5 p.m., and by appointment.

MB Roland Distillery

137 Barkers Mill Rd., Pembroke, KY 42266; (270) 640-7744
mbrdistillery.com; info@mbrdistillery.com

MB Roland is an authentic "grain-to-glass" distillery owned and operated by Paul and Merry Beth Tomaszewski (see profile). They make a wide range of spirits including True Kentucky Shine, Kentucky White Dog, Kentucky Black Dog, and different infusions (Strawberry, Blueberry, Pink Lemonade, Apple Pie, and St. Elmo's Fire). Currently distributed in nine states.

Visits: Tours given Tuesday through Saturday from 10 a.m. to 6 p.m. on the hour; call ahead for groups of ten or more.

Silver Trail Distillery

136 Palestine Rd., Hardin, KY 42048; (270) 354-6209
lblmoonshine.com; silvertraildistillery@gmail.com

Spencer Balentine pays homage to his family's moonshining heritage at this small craft distillery (see profile). At the same time, he honors the legacy of the Land Between the Lakes, a once-thriving moonshine region that was converted to a national recreation area by the federal government.

Visits: Call for appointment.

MISSOURI

Copper Run Distillery

1901 Day Rd., Walnut Shade, MO 65771; (417) 587-3456

A small artisan distillery, Copper Run is the first legal operation in the Ozark Mountains since Prohibition. They make Ozark Mountain Moonshine, an 80-proof corn whiskey. Available in Missouri only.

Visits: Tours given daily at noon, 2, 4, and 6 p.m., and include a small sampling. The tasting room has a cocktail and light food menu at reasonable prices.

Crown Valley Brewing and Distilling

13226 State Rd. F, Ste. Genevieve, MO 63670; (573) 756-9700
crowncountry.com; info@crownvalleybrewery.com

As the name implies, Crown Valley doubles as a microbrewery. They produce Missouri Moonshine, a 100-proof whiskey distilled from corn, sugar, rye, and barley, distributed within the state.

Visits: Brewery tours are available; call for distillery tour if interested.

Mad Buffalo Distillery

Shawneetown Spur, Union, MO 63084
madbuffalobrewingcompany.com; info@madbuffalodistillery.com

The family-owned Mad Buffalo Distillery is a "ground-to-glass" operation, founded in 1978 and located on Shawnee Bend Farms. They grow all the ingredients for their products and conduct their business in an environmentally responsible manner. Their Thunderbeast Storm Moonshine is a 100-proof corn whiskey, distributed locally.

Visits: Unknown.

Mid-Best Distillery

423 Valley Rd., Gravois, MO 65037; (816) 838-3139
mid-bestdistillery.com; mike@mid-bestdistillery.com
Mid-Best is a new start-up producing a handful of unaged whiskeys, including a 100-proof moonshine; currently, they have limited distribution within the state.

Visits: Unknown.

Ozark Distillery

1684 Hwy. KK, Osage Beach, MO 65065; (573) 348-2449
ozarkdistillery.com; ttaestates@charter.net
Ozark makes traditional moonshine with Missouri-grown corn; their products include a 100-proof whiskey and several infusions (including Vanilla Bean, Apple Pie, and Butterscotch). Distribution is currently within the state.

Visits: Unknown.

Montana

Willie's Distillery

312 E. Main St., Ennis, MT 59729; (406) 682-4117
williesdistillery.com; info@williesdistillery.com

Willie's is owned by Robin Blazer, who grew up on a Montana wheat farm, and his wife, Willie, who hails from the Appalachian mountains of North Carolina—a marriage made in heaven. They produce 90-proof Montana Moonshine and 70-proof Honey Moonshine; distribution is local.

Visits: Tasting room hours daily; call for details.

Nevada

Las Vegas Distillery

7330 Eastgate Rd., Unit 100, Hendersonville, NV 89001;
(702) 629-7534

lasvegasdistillery.com; info@lasvegasdistillery.com

Located twenty minutes from the Strip, Las Vegas Distillery was founded by a first-generation Hungarian family from Transylvania (only in America). Their lineup of spirits includes Nevada Moonshine, a 100-proof whiskey made from local corn, and an Apple Pie infusion. Currently distributed in Nevada and California.

Visits: Various free and paid tours offered; call for details.

7 Troughs Distilling

1155 Watson Way, Ste. 5, Sparks, NV 89431; (775) 219-9403
7troughsdistilling.com

Entrepreneur Tom Adams opened his distillery in the former Seven Troughs Mining District, where gold was discovered in 1905. He makes Recession Proof Moonshine (80 proof) from local corn and malted barley. Distribution is local.

Visits: Unknown.

NEW YORK

Clayton Distillery

40164 NY State Rd. 12, Clayton, NY 13624; (315) 285-5004
claytondistillery.com; info@claytondistillery.com

Located in the Thousand Islands region, the newly founded Clayton Distillery produces Two Dog Moonshine, a 92-proof spirit distilled from corn and other locally grown grains, on their fifth-generation family farm.

Visits: Call to verify.

Dutch's Spirits

Pine Plains, NY 12567; no contact information available

Dutch's Spirits is located on a farm supposedly owned by gangster Dutch Schultz, who ran a distillery complex there in the 1930s. The site is currently being renovated and restored, with the goal of establishing "a self-sustaining farm operation and agritourism destination specializing in artisanal hand-made spirits." Their 80-proof Sugar Wash Moonshine (made from 100 percent Demerara sugar—no corn) is available at more than 250 locations within the state, as well as through online retailers.

Visits: Not at the present time.

King's County Distillery

Brooklyn Navy Yard, Bldg. 121, 639 Flushing Ave., Brooklyn, NY 11205; no phone
kingscountydistillery.com; info@kingscountydistillery.com

More than trees are growing in Brooklyn: David Haskell and Colin Spoelman established their micro-distillery in 2010, and have established a cult following within the city. Their 80-proof Kings County Distillery Moonshine is made from Finger Lakes corn and a touch of Scottish barley, and bottled in two-hundred-milliliter flasks. Distribution within New York State only.

Visits: Tours and tastings available from 2:30 to 5:30 p.m. every Saturday; cost is $8. No reservations necessary.

Lake George Distilling Company

11262 State Rte. 149, Fort Ann, NY 12827; (518) 639-1025
lakegeorgedistillingcompany.com; info@lakegeorgedistilling
company.com

Founded in 2010, the tiny Lake George distillery makes handcrafted spirits from local grains. Among them is 32 Mile Moonshine, a corn whiskey named for the length of Lake George. Limited distribution within the state.

Visits: Contact by e-mail if interested.

Van Brunt Stillhouse

6 Bay St., 1st floor, Brooklyn, NY 11231; (718) 852-6405
vanbruntstillhouse.com; info@vanbruntstillhouse.com

Located in the Red Hook section of Brooklyn, a waterfront area that once was a hub of liquor production, Van Brunt is a new operation run by Daric Schlesselman. His New Make Moonshine Whiskey is available at locations in and around the city.

Visits: Free public tours offered on the second Sunday of each month, but do not include tastings.

North Carolina

Piedmont Distillers

3960 US Highway 220, Madison, NC 27025; (336) 445-0055
piedmontdistillers.com
Piedmont is the leader in the US moonshine category, producing nearly two of every three bottles consumed in America. They began producing Catdaddy spiced moonshine in 2005, and in 2007 launched Junior Johnson's Midnight Moon, in collaboration with the legendary NASCAR driver (see profile). The Midnight Moon line consists of the 80-proof Original, and a series of fruit infusions (Apple Pie, Cherry, Strawberry, Blueberry, Cranberry, and Blackberry) bottled at 70 proof. Distributed in most states.
Visits: Call for details.

Howling Moon Distillery

PO Box 18724, Asheville, NC 28814
howlingmoonshine.com; info@howlingmoonshine.com
Howling Moon is owned and operated by Cody Bradford and Chivous Downey, lifelong friends who are both descended from generations of moonshiners. They are committed to making an

authentic product that will replicate the experience of drinking mountain moonshine 150 years ago (see profile). They bottle an Original Moonshine along with Apple Pie and Strawberry, all at 100 proof. Currently available only in North Carolina.

Visits: None at the present time.

Troy & Sons

12 Old Charlotte Hwy., Ste. T, Asheville, NC 28803; (828) 575-2000

troyandsons.com; info@troyandsons.com

Troy Ball might be the only female moonshiner in America—a dynamo of a woman who learned the business from a collection of old-time practitioners (see profile). She makes "keeper moonshine," an heirloom product reminiscent of the liquor the moonshiners traditionally kept for themselves. Her range includes the Platinum and Oak Reserve, both 80 proof. Currently available in six states.

Visits: Tours given at 5 and 6 p.m. on Thursday, Friday, and Saturday.

PENNSYLVANIA

Mountain Top Distillery

5451 State Rte. 654, Williamsport, PA 17702; (570) 745-2332
mountaintopdistillery.com; mountaintopdistillery@gmail.com
This distillery makes a trio of corn whiskeys—Bucked Off Shine, Rode Hard Shine, and Bareback Shine—but no information was available on any of the products.
Visits: Unknown.

Mountain View Vineyard

5866 Neola Rd., Stroudsburg, PA 18360; (570) 619-0053
mountainviewvineyard.com; info@mountainviewvineyard.com
Mountain View is a winery that also produces a 100-proof corn whiskey called Original Shine, as well as a lower-proof Apple Pie.
Visits: Free distillery tours offered at 2 and 4 p.m. on Saturday and Sunday; call ahead for groups of ten or more.

Philadelphia Distilling

12285 McNulty Rd., Philadelphia, PA 19154; (215) 671-0346
shinewhiskey.com; info@shinewhiskey.com
Opened in 2005, Philadelphia Distilling was Pennsylvania's

first craft distiller since Prohibition, and became well known for spirits such as Bluecoat American Dry Gin and Vieux Carré Absinthe Supérieure. They make XXX Shine, a clear corn whiskey at 88.8 proof, and two flavored moonshines (LiberTea and Salted Caramel) at 60 proof. Currently available in eighteen states and the District of Columbia.

Visits: Call for details.

SOUTH CAROLINA

Dark Corner Distillery

241-B N. Main St., Greenville, SC 29601; (864) 631-1144
darkcornerdistillery.com

Dark Corner is a "craft micro distillery" located in Glassy Mountain Township, old stomping grounds of the outlaw Lewis Redmond. They produce a 100-proof clear corn moonshine, as well as eight flavored moonshines bottled at lower proof levels. Available in three states and the District of Columbia.

Visits: Open from noon to 6 p.m. Monday through Saturday; call ahead.

Firefly Distillery

**6775 Bears Bluff Rd., Wadmalaw Island, SC 29487;
(843) 557-1405**
fireflyvodka.com

Firefly began as a vodka producer and then branched out into
a full line of moonshine, including White Lightning at 100.7
proof and a range of flavored products (Apple Pie, Peach, Cherry,
Strawberry, etc.). Available in all fifty states and the District of
Columbia.

Visits: Tours and tastings (for a fee) offered Tuesday through
Saturday from 11 a.m. to 5 p.m., except January; call to verify.

Palmetto Moonshine

200 W. Benson St., Anderson, SC 29624; (864) 226-9917
palmettomoonshine.com; info@palmettomoonshine.com

Brothers Trey and Bryan Boggs opened their distillery in January
2011. Their products include Palmetto Moonshine, a 105-proof
corn whiskey, and three flavored moonshines (Apple Pie,
Blackberry, and Peach). They are currently distributed in three
states and the District of Columbia.

Visits: Distillery open from 10 a.m. to 7 p.m. Monday through
Saturday, and tours offered; call ahead for groups of ten or more.

TENNESSEE

Corsair Artisan Distillery

1200 Clinton St. #110, Nashville, TN 37203; (615) 200-0320
corsairartisan.com

Corsair is a brewery and distillery started by Darek Bell and Andrew Webber. They make a wide range of products, including an 85-proof Pumpkin Spiced Moonshine. A second distillery is located in Bowling Green, Kentucky.

Visits: Distillery tours and spirits tastings available every day except Monday; charge ranges $8–$10. Reserve on website.

Full Throttle

107 Parks Plaza, Trimble, TN; (731) 882-1883
fullthrottlemoonshine.com

Michael Ballard, a native of Trimble, Tennessee (population 637), is building his distillery there following his success starring in a reality TV show. He markets 80-proof Full Throttle S'loonshine, along with 70-proof infusions of Peach, Strawberry, and Apple. The distillery was scheduled for completion in the fall of 2013, and moonshine has been commercially available since the middle of 2012, made for him on a contract basis. Currently sold in eighteen states.

Visits: None at the present time.

Ole Smoky

903 Parkway, Gatlinburg, TN 37738; (865) 436-6995
olesmokymoonshine.com; shine@osdistillery.com

Ole Smoky opened on July 4, 2010, and has become a tourist destination in Gatlinburg, sponsoring tours, tastings, and events at their distillery called "The Holler." It was founded by Joe Baker, who claims that his family was among the first to set foot in the Smoky Mountains and has been moonshining ever since. Products include two clear whiskeys, Original Moonshine and White Lightnin' (both 100 proof), and a range of flavored moonshines at lower proof levels. Widespread distribution.

Visits: Open daily from 10 a.m. to 10 p.m.

Popcorn Sutton's Tennessee White Whiskey

PO Box 90371, Nashville, TN 37209
popcornsuttonswhiskey.com; info@popcornsuttonswhiskey.com

Popcorn Sutton was a legendary and controversial Appalachian moonshiner (see profile). This product, a corn whiskey bottled at 93 proof, has been controversial as well. It was created after Sutton's suicide as a joint venture between his widow and Hank Williams Jr.; the distiller is Jamey Grosser, who is identified as Popcorn's apprentice and friend. According to some sources, the recipe is not authentic, and Grosser had no connection with

Sutton. The location of the distillery is unknown. Currently available in four states.

Visits: None.

Prichard's Distillery

12 Kelso Smithland Rd., Kelso, TN 37348; (931) 433-5454
prichardsdistillery.com
Phil Prichard, descended from five generations of distillers, opened his operation in 1997. He makes a wide range of products including Lincoln County Lightning, a 90-proof clear corn whiskey. Widely distributed.

Visits: Free tours offered Monday through Friday from 9 a.m. to 3 p.m. and Saturday from 9 a.m. to 2 p.m.

Short Mountain Distillery

119 Mountain Spirits Ln., Woodbury, TN 37190; (615) 216-0830
shortmountaindistillery.com
Short Mountain is owned by the Kaufman brothers, owners of a three-hundred-acre farm aiming for organic certification; their moonshine is made by Ricky Estes and Ronald Lawson, who once plied their trade illicitly up in the hills. They make 105-proof Short Mountain Tennessee Moonshine, along with a lower-proof Apple Pie. Available from the distillery and online retailers.

Visits: Free tours and tastings offered; call for current schedule.

Virginia

Belmont Farms Distillery

13490 Cedar Run Rd., Culpeper, VA 22701; (540) 825-3207
belmontfarmdistillery.com

Belmont Farms is owned by Chuck and Jeanette Miller, who grow the ingredients for their products on their 195-acre spread. They make Virginia Lightning, a 100-proof corn whiskey, as well as lower-proof Apple Pie and Cherry infusions. According to the website, their products are available in nine states and the District of Columbia. They also make Stillhouse Moonshine on a contract basis (see below).

Visits: Free tours offered every fifteen minutes when the distillery is open; tastings cost $5. Call to verify hours.

Stillhouse Distillery

moonshine.com; info@moonshine.com

Stillhouse is a partnership between Steve McPherson and "serial entrepreneur" Brad Beckerman. They entered into a partnership with Chuck Miller of Belmont Farms, who handcrafts the product in his copper pot stills using estate-grown corn. Their Original Moonshine is a clear corn whiskey bottled at 80 proof and currently available in seven states.

Visits: See Belmont Farms.

Tim Smith Moonshine

Climax, VA

climaxmoonshine.com; info@prostbevco.com

Tim Smith, made famous by the *Moonshiners* TV show, is selling his 90-proof Climax Moonshine in five states. The whiskey has reportedly been made for him on a contract basis, although he is currently building a distillery.

Visits: None at the present time.

Virginia Sweetwater Distillery

760 Walkers Creek Rd., Marion, VA, 24354; (276) 378-0867

virginiawhiskeys.com

Scott Schumaker operates Appalachian Mountain Spirits LLC on his farm, crafting liquor from local ingredients. Among his products is Virginia Sweetwater Moonshine, an 85-proof corn whiskey. Currently distributed within Virginia.

Visits: Tours offered by appointment Monday through Saturday from 10 a.m. to 5 p.m.; send request via website.

WASHINGTON

2bar Spirits

2960 4th Ave. South, Seattle, WA 98134; (206) 402-4340
2barspirits.com

Five generations of Nathan Kaiser's family were farmers in South Texas. After relocating to Seattle, he makes 2bar Spirits Moonshine, bottled at 80 proof and distributed within the state.

Visits: Free tastings offered daily from 2 to 6 p.m.

Batch 206 Distillery

1417 Elliott Ave. West, Seattle, WA 98119; (206) 216-2803
batch206.com

Owner Jeff Steichen set up shop after Washington enacted its craft distillery legislation in 2008. His See 7 Stars Moonshine is a 100-proof corn whiskey made with a recipe sourced from the South Carolina hills, produced from Columbia Basin corn and Washington malted barley. It is available in Oregon, and in Washington direct from the distillery.

Visits: Unknown; call to verify.

Deception Distilling

9946 Padilla Heights Rd., Anacortes, WA 98221; (360) 588-1000
deceptiondistilling.com; deceptiondistilling@hotmail.com

Deception Distilling was founded in 2012 by Harold Christenson, a local craftsman who commissioned a copper still from the German manufacturer Arnold Holstein. Among his products is Skagit Moon Corn Whiskey, a 100-proof small-batch moonshine currently available within the state.

Visits: Tastings offered Monday through Friday from 8 a.m. to 4:30 p.m. and Saturday from 8 a.m. to 2:30 p.m.

It's 5 Artisan Distillery

101 Maple St., Cashmere, WA 98815; (509) 679-9771
its5distillery.com

The It's 5 Artisan Distillery (as in "it's five o'clock somewhere") is owned by Colin Levi. They produce a range of spirits, including a clear corn-based moonshine and a liquor called Sunshine (moonshine aged in charred oak barrels). The distribution is limited to Washington State.

Visits: Tours every hour Monday through Friday from noon to 4 p.m. and Saturday from 1 to 4 p.m.

Mount Baker Distillery

1305 Fraser St., Ste. D2, Bellingham, WA 98229; (360) 734-3301
mountbakerdistillery.com

This distillery produces Mount Baker Moonshine, a 100-proof whiskey distilled from Washington State corn and available for purchase within the state.

Visits: Tours offered; call for appointment.

West Virginia

Hatfield & McCoy Moonshine

PO Box 1716, Gilbert, WV 25621; (304) 687-3340
drinkofthedevil.com; nancy@drinkofthedevil.com
Thanks to the History Channel, a large chunk of the public
now knows about the feud between the Hatfields and McCoys,
which continued for nearly three decades and claimed more than
one dozen lives. This distillery is run by Nancy Hatfield, great-
great-granddaughter of Devil Anse Hatfield, one of the men
who started it all, along with her son-in-law Chad Bishop. Their
handcrafted, 90-proof moonshine is distributed within West
Virginia.

Visits: Unknown.

Isiah Morgan Distillery

45 Winery Ln., Summersville, WV 26651; (888) 4WV-WINE
(498-9463)
Isiah Morgan is a micro-distillery (the nation's smallest,
supposedly) founded by the late Rodney Facemire and located at
the Kirkwood Winery. They make a moonshine called Southern
Moon, available only at the property.

Visits: Tours and tastings offered; call for schedule.

Pinchgut Hollow Distillery

1602 Tulip Ln., Fairmont, WV 26554; (304) 366-WINE (9463)
hestonfarm.com

Pinchgut Hollow is a craft distillery located on the winery grounds of Heston Farm. They make two moonshines (Buckwheat Moon and CornShine), both 100 proof, along with Honey Peach Moon and Apple Pie Shine. Their products are distributed locally.

Visits: Call for details.

West Virginia Distilling Company

1380 Fenwick Ave., Morgantown, WV 26505; (304) 599-0960
mountainmoonshine.com; pfireman@frontier.com

Payton Fireman, an attorney with many hobbies, founded the tiny West Virginia Distilling Co. in 1999. He produces Mountain Moonshine, a 100-proof corn whiskey sold in licensed West Virginia state liquor stores.

Visits: Call for details.

Index

health hazards
  ethylene glycol (antifreeze),
    81, 202
  lead poisoning, 81
  methanol (methyl alcohol/
    wood alcohol), 78, 81
Henderson, John B., 25
Herrick, Myron T., 44, 46
Higgins, Howard, 198
Hiram Walker and Sons
    (distillery), 41–42, 51–52
Hogeland, William, 7
Howling Moon Distillery.
    See also Bradford, Cody;
    Downey, Chivous
  beginnings of, 190–194
  description and contact
    information, 240–241
  drink recipes, 204–206
  expansion and future
    growth, 202–203
Hutcheson, Neal, 211

I

Illinois, present-day
    distilleries, 231
income tax, 18, 19, 46, 53, 55

Internal Revenue Service
    (IRS, formerly Bureau
    of Internal Revenue), 31,
    34, 48
Iowa, present-day
    distilleries, 231

J

Jack Daniel Distillery, 221
Jefferson, Thomas, 13, 16
Jester, Tom Wilson, 214, 217
Jim Beam (whiskey), 18
Johns, Art, 52
Johnson, Andrew
    (president), 23
Johnson, Charles M., 60
Johnson, Dwayne ("The
    Rock"), 97
Johnson, Glenn ("Junior")
  on birth of NASCAR,
    116–120, 132–134
  on early bootlegging days,
    127–132
  on moonshine costs and
    taxation, 83
  on NASCAR safety and
    innovation, 121–123

About the Author

Mark Spivak is an award-winning writer specializing in wine, spirits, food, restaurants, and culinary travel. He was the wine writer for the *Palm Beach Post* from 1994 to 1999, and was honored by the Academy of Wine Communications for excellence in wine coverage "in a graceful and approachable style." Since 2001 he has been the wine and spirits editor for the Palm Beach Media Group, as well as the restaurant critic for *Palm Beach Illustrated*. His work has appeared in *National Geographic Traveler*, *Robb Report*, *Art & Antiques*, *Men's Journal*, the *Continental* and *Ritz-Carlton* magazines, *Arizona Highways*, and *Newsmax*. A broadcaster for many years, Mark is currently working with Matrix Media to host *Quench!*, a weekly podcast that reveals the untold stories behind everyone's favorite alcoholic beverages, available on iTunes and at webtalkradio.net. He is the author of *Iconic Spirits: An Intoxicating History*.